STEPHEN PLATTEN

ABBEYS & PRIORIES OF BRITAIN

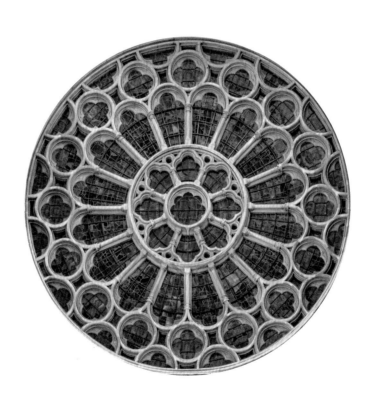

Publication in this form © 2022 Pitkin Publishing
An imprint of B.T. Batsford Holdings Limited

Written by Stephen Platten

The author has asserted his moral rights.

No part of this publication may be reproduced,
stored in a retrieval system or transmitted in any
form or by any means without the permission of
Pitkin Publishing and the copyright holders.

ISBN: 978-1-84165-938-1   1/22

Printed in Turkey

Pitkin Publishing, B.T. Batsford Holdings Limited
43 Great Ormond Street, London WC1N 3HZ
www.batsford.com +44 (0)20 7462 1506

Edited by Clare Sayer
Designed by Geoff Borin

Front cover: Fountains Abbey.
Back cover: Wymondham Abbey (top),
Holyrood Abbey (bottom).
Right: Whitby Abbey, viewed from the east.

Editor's note: Both 'choir' and the variant spelling 'quire'
have been used in accordance with the wishes of the individual
cathedrals concerned.

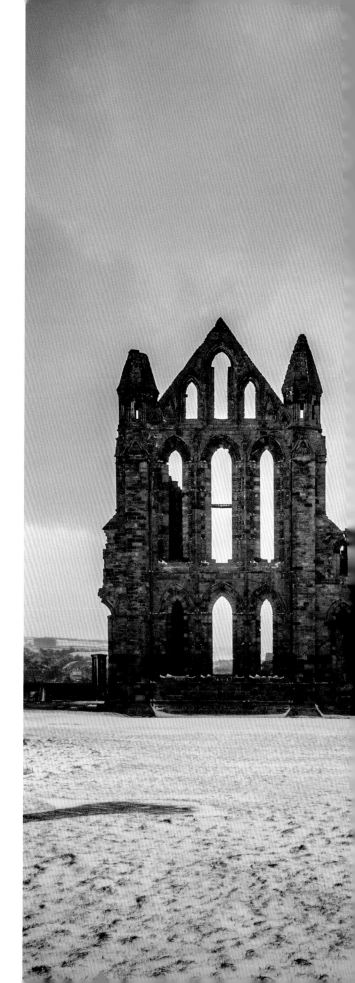

CONTENTS

Above: St Augustine's Abbey in Canterbury, with the Cathedral's 'Bell Harry Tower' in the background.

INTRODUCTION

KINGDOMS OF KINGDOMS

The Kingdoms of Scotland and England and the Principality of Wales – just like the languages they now speak – are the products of a remarkable tapestry of different strands, comprising the earlier kingdoms which gradually formed the union we now know. Each of those traditions contributed to the growth of the religious life and the artistic and architectural development of the buildings within which the religious lived. It is for that reason that this book uses those early kingdoms as section titles, to suggest these early roots.

The impact of the religious life upon our nations is often not recognised. Oxbridge colleges cluster around courts and quads hinting at the cloisters which pre-dated them; monasteries were laboratories for learning; Cistercian houses were often built close to ore deposits and also had large granges to accommodate sheep and cattle – monks were pioneers of industry and farming. All this stands alongside their crucial religious significance. This indicates both the power and the influence of religious orders in the making of European civilisation. The roots of this tradition go back well beyond the growth of European self-consciousness – even beyond the roots of Christianity. The Dead Sea Scrolls and the culture they represent, for example, issued from a second-century Jewish monastery-like complex, indicating that a corporate religious lifestyle existed well before the beginnings of Christianity.

EARLY CHRISTIAN COMMUNITIES

In the fourth century, St Antony in Egypt and St Jerome in Judaea, and later the Desert Fathers, pioneered a form of solitary monasticism that survives in Egypt and Ethiopia down to the present day. Monks lived secluded lives in separate cells that were constructed around a central church, coming together only for common worship. A similar style of religious life existed in those places where Irish Christian discipleship was the main instrument of

mission. In the rural and remote areas of Ireland, and then later in Iona and in Cornwall, solitaries would build cells around a simple church. They would use these centres as bases for missionary forays into the surrounding countryside. In the seventh century, Aidan was sent from Iona to Lindisfarne as a missionary to the kingdom of Northumbria; he again established an Irish-style monastery as his base. There were similar religious centres in Wales, and at least one in East Anglia.

Then, in the early seventh century, Augustine established his missionary centre in Canterbury, in the kingdom of Kent, with later missionaries moving on to Rochester and London. Augustine had been sent to England by Pope Gregory the Great, himself a monk. By this time, the influence of St Benedict, who had died in the mid sixth century, was already beginning to make its mark. Benedict, an Italian, is seen as the father of Western monasticism. He, and his Rule, more than anything else, began to give shape and stability to that form of monasticism which was lived in community. His rule is a remarkable balance of guidelines for wholesome living and challenges to live the Christian life. The pattern of life that issued from the Benedictine way would become formalised in the shape and structure of the monastic complex. It is this which helps us to understand the British abbeys and priories that have survived, either completely or as ruins.

The growth of the religious life in medieval times is often not fully appreciated. For example, at the beginning of the twelfth century in England alone, the numbers of such foundations could be counted on the fingers of one's hands; by the end of the twelfth century there were more than 300 religious houses scattered across the country. The sheer explosion of monasticism is demonstrated by glancing at maps which indicate their numerical presence. In 1950, the Ordnance Survey published two extraordinarily informative sheets titled simply *Map of Monastic Britain*. These two sheets still repay careful study and open up a new world for any who live within these shores.

THE MONASTIC TRADITION

At the heart of the religious life stands the discipline of prayer and thus the monastic church is the focus in every abbey and priory. In the choir, the monks would gather for prayer at least seven times in every twenty-four hours; they would even rise during the middle of the night to pray, the night stair down to the church survives in places. Beyond the space known as the choir, which was normally at the heart of the church, to the east would be the high altar, around which the monks or sisters would gather for mass. To the west of the choir, generally beyond a wooden or stone screen, was the nave, or people's church, where mass would be sung with and for the local population, possibly also with pilgrims, and in some cases with the 'lay brothers' of the community. The monks would generally live in dormitories (dorters) and they would eat corporately in large hall-like refectories. There would be a guest house for pilgrims and travellers, and often a hostry (a pilgrims' hall) where travellers would be welcomed. These monastic buildings would also include a chapter house for conventual meetings and a library. These

would be ranged around a cloister. The cloister was thus the nexus of all routes, the crossroads of the monastery. It stood at the heart of a stable, contemplative community – the Benedictine rule includes a vow of stability. The monks were encouraged to stay within the bounds of the monastery and not to be wanderers – Benedict has harsh words to say about peripatetic monks, whom he calls gyrovagues!

As the Middle Ages progressed, so other orders developed. In the twelfth century, a stricter interpretation of the Benedictine vows, pioneered at Cîteaux in southern France, gave birth to the Cistercian order. The asceticism here was harsher and the geographical position of the monasteries generally remote – Fountains and Valle Crucis Abbeys are but two examples. Cistercians pioneered efficient farming and, as working communities, survived by including within their number numerous lay brothers, who helped run the monastery and the farms. It is not an exaggeration to say that the Benedictines (with the Cistercians) were perhaps more responsible than any other group of people for the foundation and self-understanding of medieval Europe. The culture of learning and the importance of the leadership of the abbot was seminal in the growth of European civilisation.

Still other religious orders developed. The mendicant (those forbidden to own property) orders of friars, that is, the Franciscans or Greyfriars, the Dominicans or Blackfriars, and the Carmelites or Whitefriars – all were founded at the end of the twelfth and beginning of the thirteenth centuries. These orders were missionary and so mobile in contrast to the Benedictines. Groups of secular and Augustinian canons also came to live in community. Different again were the Carthusians; the 'charterhouses', in which they lived bore some similarities to early monasticism. The monks lived in separate houses and came together only for community worship. Mount Grace Priory in Yorkshire is a fine example of this expression of the religious life. In England, uniquely, a number of the medieval cathedrals were also priories in themselves.

ARCHITECTURAL DEVELOPMENT

The style of architecture of English priories and abbeys developed at the same time as the communities who inhabited them. The simplicity of Saxon architecture, often with fairly primitive round-headed arches and windows, gave way to

Left: Mount Grace Priory.

Above: Rievaulx Abbey.

the austere strength of the Romanesque style. Romanesque took its name from the solid round arcades and strong pillars which had developed from Roman architecture. In Britain this style is primarily associated with the Norman invaders and is often simply styled Norman. Tewkesbury Abbey is an excellent example of this style.

In the late Romanesque period, the arches began to become pointed and this style is often termed Transitional. In the late twelfth and early thirteenth centuries, Romanesque eventually gave way to the lighter touch of Early English, focused on the familiar three slender and parallel lancets seen at Rievaulx and at Whitby. Early English marks the beginnings of medieval English Gothic, which matured into the intricacy of the Decorated and Geometric tracery familiar in so many English parish churches. Among abbeys and priories, the nave of Beverley Minster is a fine example. The apotheosis of English Gothic is reached in the Perpendicular period, during the fifteenth and sixteenth centuries, with its strong vertical lines and sumptuous fan vaulting. The Henry

VII Chapel in Westminster Abbey and St George's Chapel, Windsor are perfect examples.

The Renaissance led eventually to the rediscovery of the principles of Classical architecture, and the seventeenth and eighteenth centuries saw a flowering of the Classical style, but with the Reformation, the power and strength of the monastic life was suppressed and eclipsed. The nineteenth century saw a rediscovery of medievalism, albeit in a most creative manner, in the work of the great Victorian architects, but again here it would have little influence, except perhaps in the restoration of earlier buildings where they had survived. This remarkable development of architectural styles and expression is just one part of the background to the abbeys and priories to which this book seeks to introduce you.

THE KINGDOM OF NORTHUMBRIA

Northumbria began as two kingdoms: Deira from the Humber to the Tees and Bernicia from the Tees into what is now southern Scotland. Lothian remained part of Northumbria after King (later Saint) Oswald's victory at Heavenfield in 633 when Deira and Bernicia became a united Northumbria, only becoming part of Scotland after the Battle of Carham in 1018. Northumbria became an early crucible of Christian culture. Lindisfarne, Jarrow, Bishopwearmouth and Durham are part of the surviving evidence of this. This huge swathe of northern England thus owes much of its monastic heritage to the Northumbrian inheritance. The later abbeys and priories at Lindisfarne, Whitby, Hexham, Ripon and Durham Cathedral are direct descendants. Sadly, much has disappeared – Berwick-upon-Tweed had fifteen religious houses of differing observances and functions – barely one stone survives. In Alnwick, only the abbey gatehouse, buildings from the Carmelite priory in Hulne Park, and fragments of a lazar house (lepers' colony) speak of this past. The crypts at Hexham, Ripon and Lastingham are other early survivals, linked with St Wilfrid and St Cedd. Nonetheless, of the explosion of the religious life in the twelfth century, much remains for the visitor, tourist and pilgrim.

KIRKSTALL ABBEY

Kirkstall can boast two or three eccentricities which verge on the unique. First of all, it is the best preserved of all the English monasteries. Second, until 1827, the lane connecting Leeds with Skipton passed through the church running from east to west, with the east wall and the east window being removed for just that purpose; the new road avoided that but still separated the abbey from its gatehouse, which stands on the corner of Abbey Walk opposite, and is now the Abbey House Museum. Finally, Kirkstall's elevation was included in Josiah Wedgwood's celebrated and vast 'Frog' china service commissioned by Catherine the Great of Russia – fame indeed.

Remarkably it survives as a striking sight only two miles from the centre of Leeds. Begun originally at Barnoldswick in 1147, the monks and lay brothers were able to obtain this site in the Aire valley in 1152, which they named Kirkstall. It would appear that the main buildings were complete before the death of Alexander, the first abbot, in 1182; the church was finished five years earlier. There was some additional building in the early thirteenth century, and in the late fifteenth/early sixteenth century new kitchens were constructed.

Kirkstall, a Cistercian house, was founded from Fountains and there are clear similarities. The church, which is all of one date, was built to what was at that time the standard Cistercian design. With a long nave and short presbytery, there are two aisled transepts, each with three chapels to the east. There is a great central tower, again like Fountains built in the sixteenth century, not long before the Dissolution – sadly the collapse of the western arch of the crossing brought down the west and north sides of the tower. The south and half of the east remain – it is a perilous sight. Rather remarkably the rib vaulting of the presbytery survives. The west front of the church is austere Romanesque.

Alongside this, much of the cloister court is still there. On the west side stands the inner wall of the lay brothers' range. Next to the south transept, the library was converted in the early nineteenth century into a grotto/summerhouse. Next to this is the noble double-arched entrance to the Chapter House; next door once again is the vaulted parlour. From here a passageway leads to the former infirmary, now visible only as foundations. The visitor centre in the lay brothers' reredorter was built in 2006 by Purcell, Miller and Tritton.

Following the Dissolution, Kirkstall survived with less damage than many other monasteries for a variety of different reasons. First it was farmed, but with comparatively minor demolition. Then, in the nineteenth century, Colonel John North acquired the Cardigan estate, of which the abbey was part, and gave it to the city corporation. This process of consolidation had been helped by the abbey becoming a favourite subject for artists including Girtin, Corman and Turner.

Opposite: Looking west to Lindisfarne Priory and village.
Right: A view of the partially ruined tower.

BEVERLEY MINSTER

Beverley is a town of two glorious churches: St Mary's, the ancient parish church set near to the centre of the town, and the Minster lying further towards the southern edge. St Mary's was originally a daughter church of the minster, the minster having a very long history, with a major church on this site from as early as *c.*700. In his *Ecclesiastical History of England*, Bede refers to the monastery founded at Beverley by Bishop John of York. Refounded as a collegiate church of secular canons in the tenth century, it gained greatly in significance with the canonisation of Bishop John as St John of Beverley in 1037, and the development of his cult.

From the mid eleventh century onwards, the church was rebuilt in the Romanesque style. Following a fire in 1188, and the collapse of the central tower in 1213, the church underwent further reconstruction starting around 1220, with the king giving forty oaks from Sherwood Forest towards the rebuilding. The new minster was conceived on cathedral scale, with double transepts like Lincoln. Rebuilding began at the east end with the fine Early English work in the retrochoir, choir and transepts. The nave was begun *c.*1311 in the Decorated style and completed in the 1390s, although work may have been halted in 1348–9 on account of the Black Death. Another gift of oaks was received in 1388 with an indulgence being granted for new work in 1408. This allowed the Perpendicular western towers

to be added and the nave to be completed. The west front includes the arms of Richard II. The fifteenth-century north porch is monumental. Only the Percy Chapel (*c.*1490) and the choir stalls (*c.*1520) came later. Outstanding furnishings include the tomb of Lady Eleanor Percy (*c.*1340), perhaps the most splendid of all such Decorated monuments in England. The choir stalls, with sixty-eight misericords, include the largest collection in England of carved figures playing medieval musical instruments. Nicholas Hawksmoor surveyed the minster in 1716–7 and thereafter directed the restoration, which was completed under William Thornton in 1730. Hawksmoor was also responsible for the crossing tower of 1721.

There is a mixed collection of stained glass, with the thirteenth- to fifteenth-century work now all grouped together in the east window. In 2004 an exceptional scheme of contemporary stained glass by Helen Whittaker on the theme of Pilgrimage was added in the retrochoir. Scott, in his restoration, designed the decoration above the choir. As with Hexham Abbey there is a frithstool-style throne, possible from as early as the seventh century; originally it would have been sited in the apse as with the throne in Norwich Cathedral. The font canopy and carved panels on the west door are superb, and there is also a very fine bishop's throne, even though at the Reformation the minster was not chosen to be the centre of a see.

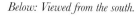

Below: Viewed from the south.

BYLAND ABBEY

n its early days, Byland was a conflicted place with serious disputes involving four other monastic communities, including two as far away as Cumbria. Much of this was on account of finding an acceptable location. Alongside that, the community had begun as a Savigniac house in Furness in 1134, and as the community was making their third move, the Savigniac order merged with the Cistercians. Thus, on this fourth attempt, in 1177, and repeating their earlier attempt to settle at Byland, this would be where they would remain, despite its close proximity to Rievaulx.

Byland is one of the finest abbey ruins in England, since the north side of the nave survives for its entire length, along with the west end and south transept corner. The original building was for some thirty-six monks and one hundred lay brothers. The remarkable spaciousness of the church as we now encounter it issues from the fact that all the piers have been lost. Following all the false starts, the church was built in the more advanced Cistercian style, which was modelled on the plans of French cathedrals of that time, with an eastern apse, an ambulatory and radiating chapels. This is similar to the plan of Abbey Dore in Herefordshire, and follows, to some degree, the pattern at Cîteaux itself. This pattern is clear from the ruins of the eastern end of the building. There will have been a triforium and a clerestory. The transepts have east and west aisles and the evidence suggests Transitional style with pointed arches. There will have been a pulpitum screen between the nave and choir and the remains of the crossing piers show

their extraordinary strength and proportions. The west front is splendid with three lancets set below a large rose window which would have then been crowned by a gable.

We can trace the pattern of the cloister which appears to have been built in two phases, beginning with the south range. The west range included the quarters of the lay brethren, with the dormitory on the upper floor and store rooms beneath; the reredorter, that is the lavatories, were at the southern end of the west range. The cloister was rebuilt in the fifteenth century, and the solid screen walls date from that period of construction. The south range, as usual, comprised the refectory, kitchen and warming house, with a mighty fireplace in its west wall. The east range beginning at the south transept was the monks' quarters with the dormitory above. The lowest steps of the night stair survive. Next comes the chapter house, then the parlatorium. Further along was the monk's reredorter. To the west of this were the abbot's lodgings with the infirmary to the south-east.

The gatehouse to the whole abbey complex is some distance to the west. Under the care of English Heritage, and with significant buildings surviving, Byland makes a perfect twin visit with nearby Rievaulx.

Above: The west front of Byland Abbey.

LINDISFARNE PRIORY

The stakes which stride out over the sands from Beal, on the mainland, towards Lindisfarne, mark the path taken by countless pilgrims over almost fourteen centuries to this unforgettable and visionary place. The castle (originally one of a ring of fortresses built by King Henry VIII, and later converted into a small country house) and the remains of the twelfth-century Benedictine abbey set the scene. Indeed, the 'Holy Island' of Lindisfarne still retains a similar atmosphere to that bestowed upon it by the early missionary saints who first founded a monastery here.

It was St Aidan who came earliest, in 635, founding a church and diocese close by to the great royal fortress at Bamburgh. Its castle too is set like that of Lindisfarne, on its own spur of volcanic whinstone. Aidan travelled from Iona at the request of Oswald, the Northumbrian king, who would also later be canonised. From here, Aidan travelled out into the surrounding wild countryside, as it was then, to assist Oswald in helping to found what became the Christian kingdom of Northumbria. Aidan acted as a counsellor to the king who, in turn, acted as translator

for Aidan who spoke only Gaelic. Bede, the great historian of the Anglo-Saxon church wrote of Aidan: 'He gave his clergy an inspiring example of self-discipline and continence, and the highest recommendation of his teaching to all was that he and his followers lived as they taught.'

Lindisfarne's aura of holiness increased further with the reputation of St Cuthbert, the great Anglo-Saxon missionary bishop, who died and was buried here in 687. Cuthbert had trained in the novitiate at the monastery of Old Melrose (founded by St Aidan), under the tutelage of St Boisil, who gave his name to the modern town of St Boswells. Cuthbert often retired to lonely places for solitary prayer and the tiny island near to the harbour is still known as St Cuthbert's Isle, after the saint's time there. Aidan's 'Irish'-style monastery would have comprised simple wooden huts for the monks, grouped around the conventual church. We do not know the exact location of the earliest monastery. In this early period, Northumbria was one of the cradles of European Christianity, as the surviving evidence of the culture – notably St Cuthbert's Cross and the Lindisfarne Gospels – indicates.

Eighth-century Viking invasions destroyed the monastic church and the community fled. It was not until the twelfth century, that century of the great flowering of the religious life, that the monastery was refounded by the Benedictine community that kept Cuthbert's shrine in Durham. It is the remains of this church which we see today. Dominating the ruins is the splendid 'rainbow arch', one of the surviving ribs of the great stone vault over the crossing. Like Durham Cathedral, the church was vaulted in stone throughout and, also like Durham, the monks built the nave using alternate cylindrical and composite Romanesque columns. The church was begun *c.*1130 and the richly decorated western doorway and surviving south-western tower date from *c.*1150. The west front collapsed towards the end of the nineteenth century but was restored on account of a generous gift of the former owner of the site. The church was completed before the monastic buildings were begun, probably *c.*1200. The apsidal chancel was extended in the twelfth century to produce a square end; here would have been the high altar and possibly the shrine of St Cuthbert. The shape of the original apsidal end is traced out in stone within the eastern arm of the church.

Left: The 'rainbow arch'.

Above: Viewed from the south-west.

The building of the monastic complex began in the western range. The pattern of the monastery is still clearly discernible, grouped around the cloister garth. On the eastern side are the massive remains of the Prior's Lodging, fortified in the fourteenth century. The outer monastic court is still unusually well preserved. Within the outer court is a moving effigy of Cuthbert in bronze by the Northumbrian sculptor, Fenwick Lawson.

There is a very good English Heritage visitor centre, which traces the history of early Northumbrian Christianity, reminding the visitor that this was where the amazing Lindisfarne Gospels (now held in the British Museum) were originally scripted. These are among the most beautiful, ancient and precious of any early manuscripts in England. Next door is the attractive thirteenth-century parish church, within which is set another very moving Fenwick Lawson

sculpture – this time it is of the monks carrying Cuthbert's coffin, in its remarkable journeying, throughout the north of England and the Borders, and eventually ending with his burial in the eleventh century in the cathedral in Durham. In the churchyard is a noble statue of Aidan by Kathleen Parbury.

The site is stunning, with the castle on an outcrop of the Great Whin Sill and the sands, covered at high tide, preserving the priory's island haven.

HEXHAM ABBEY

The abbey at Hexham returns the pilgrim to the beginnings of English Christianity and the origins of the Christian kingdom of Northumbria. King Oswald's victory at the Battle of Heavenfield, nearby, marked the start of a new era. Oswald, who would later himself be canonised, asked the monks of Iona to send missionaries to help convert Northumbria to Christianity. Aidan, the key missionary, set up his monastery and later the bishop's see at Lindisfarne. He and Cuthbert were the founding fathers of the Northumbrian church. Wilfrid was perhaps the key representative of the next generation of missionaries. Dynamic and ruthless, where he deemed it necessary, he was one of the influential personalities at the Synod of Whitby which brought together the Irish and Roman traditions. A missionary to the South Saxons as well as the Northumbrians, he was exiled more than once on account of his acerbic personality.

About 671 Queen Etheldreda, the wife of King Ecgfrith of Northumbria, gave land to Wilfrid to build a monastery. Wilfrid, according to Eddius, his biographer, built a church incomparable with any other this side of the Alps. It was, he noted, 'supported by various columns and many side aisles . . . surrounded by various winding passages with spiral stairs leading up and down'. Wilfrid, who later became Bishop of York, built his church, as a Benedictine foundation, between c.675–680 and, remarkably, the crypt of this church survives virtually intact; excavations have revealed what has been interpreted as an apsidal chapel to the east of the crypt. Hexham remained the centre of a bishop's see from 681–821. Hexham suffered severely from Danish raids and most cripplingly from those in 876, the country to the north having been ravaged by the Danes in the previous year.

The history of Hexham in the next three centuries is largely unknown and it was not until 1113, that Thomas, Archbishop of York, refounded the abbey as an priory for Augustinian canons. It was rebuilt with a nave aisled only on the north side as indeed it is today – the only surviving evidence of this is in the western respond of the aisle. The nave was again rebuilt in the fifteenth century but only its western and southern walls are extant. The chancel

Below: Looking east towards the chancel screen.

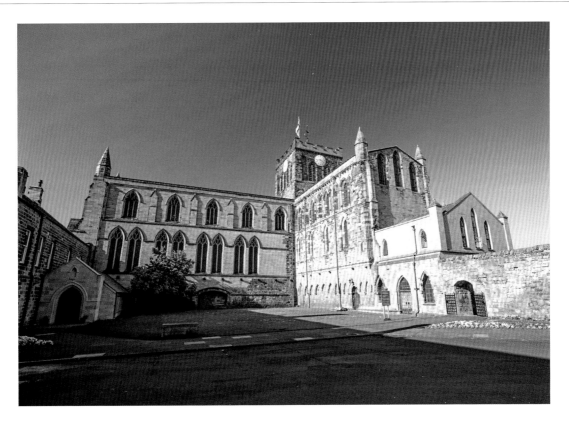

Above: Hexham Abbey with the ruins of the cloister in the foreground.

and transepts are Early English in style and were constructed in the twelfth and thirteenth centuries. Indeed, as we see it today, the church is from two periods, between 1180–1250 and then 1850–1910. Of the Saxon building, only the crypt, mentioned above, now remains. This can be compared with Wilfrid's crypt at Ripon Cathedral.

The abbey is entered through the slype – originally the passage between the cloister and the monastic cemetery. At Hexham, the slype is enclosed as the final bay of the south transept (this unusual feature is similar to the arrangement of the slype at the cathedral in Oxford). The surviving night stair – uniquely preserved here – led the monks from their dormitory to the abbey church for the office of Nocturns, which was sung in the middle of the night; it is perhaps the most monumental of English medieval stairs and is highly evocative of the former monastic life of prayer within the priory church.

To the west is the nave rebuilt in the Decorated style between 1907 and 1909 by the architect Temple Moore. This is a triumph of sensitive modern Gothic work where the gentle Decorated style avoids pastiche but nonetheless makes the nave feel integral to the overall design and internal massing of the church. The chancel dates from about 1180, although the lower courses of a Saxon apse have been exposed. One enters the chancel through a unique closed

wooden pulpitum with a loft built in the early sixteenth century by Prior Thomas Smythson. The Saxon frithstool, of *c.*675–680, is simply a stone chair probably constructed as a bishop's throne, and carved out of one piece of stone; it is unlikely that originally it sat in this position but possibly within the eastern apse of the Saxon building. It is paralleled in England only by that in Beverley Minster.

In the south transept is a Roman tombstone of Flavinus *c.*98, reminding one of nearby Hadrian's Wall and the Roman town at Corbridge. Flavinus is portrayed in full dress uniform as the standard bearer of the crack cavalry regiment, known as *Ala Petriana*. The stone was found in 1881 during work on the church. Opposite is the Acca Cross, from the grave of Bishop Acca *c.*740. The cross is attractively carved with a plant scroll and bunches of berries; remarkably the motifs are similar to carvings on the tie beams on the Dome of the Rock in Jerusalem. The cloister, as in most monastic houses, lay south of the nave and elements of it can still be seen. The lavatorium (*c.*1300), where the monks washed their hands on their way into the refectory, is still intact with its seven gabled blank arches. A reconstruction of some of the monastic buildings, completed in 2014, hosts an interesting historical exhibition about the abbey and there is further space for other presentations.

BOLTON ABBEY

S tanding within a broad sweep of the River Wharfe, Bolton Abbey has an incomparable setting. In 1155 Alicia de Romilly, of Skipton Castle, established an Augustinian priory here. In the ruins, within a broad part of the chancel of the old priory church, Romanesque blind arcading dating from *c.*1170 is still visible. Work ceased for fifty years and was resumed in the mid thirteenth century with the construction of the nave in the Early English style. The west front, which dates from this period, is highly ornate with a very fine west door. The most striking feature visible now is the incomplete western tower, which was begun in 1520 but discontinued at the Dissolution of the Monasteries. It was not until 1984 that it was roofed to form a western porch. The fine wooden roofing of the nave was begun by Prior Moone who was responsible for the western tower. The six windows on the south are all by Augustus W.N. Pugin and date from 1853. The church is set within the estate of the Duke of Devonshire and nearby are the treacherous rapids known as Bolton Strid, which have sadly claimed many victims who have tried crossing the river at this point.

Above: Looking south towards Bolton Abbey.

S et exquisitely in a wooded glen, within a loop of the River Coquet in Northumberland, this Augustinian priory was established *c.*1130–35 by William Bertram, Baron of Mitford. The church survives almost completely due to the remarkable restoration by Thomas Austin in 1858–59; the Cadogan family funded the work. Earlier, Archdeacon Thomas Sharp, son of John Sharp, Archbishop of York, attempted a reconstruction but was blocked by a row between William Fenwick and the Vicar of Felton. Despite its ruinous state, sufficient remained to make the restoration faithful to the original structure, except for the south-west corner of the nave. The style is Transitional, with a nave of six bays, aisled only on the north side. It was built *c.*1190–1220. There is a tower which hardly projects beyond the roof ridges.

Of the three nave doorways, the grandest is the north side door with a dazzling mixture of Norman ornamentation, including chevrons, zig zag and beakheads; there is also dogtoothing along the angles. There are processional doors which led to the cloister on the south. The church has a certain austerity on account of the lack of furnishing. Very little of the conventual buildings remain, although some elements were incorporated into the adjacent Manor House built for the Fenwick family and extended by John Dobson 1830–1837.

Right: The nave arcading

BRINKBURN PRIORY

BLANCHLAND ABBEY

Blanchland is unique, inasmuch as the village itself is effectively a rebuilding of the former abbey. It was transformed by the trustees of Lord Crewe's Charity, which had been set up by Lord Crewe, who was Bishop of Durham for the best part of fifty years, at the turn of the seventeenth century.

The Premonstratensian abbey was originally established in 1165 by Walter de Bolbec ll and was a daughter house of Croxton Abbey in Leicestershire. It attained full abbey status by the late thirteenth century. Blanchland had a difficult time during the fourteenth century when the abbey's granges were pillaged by the Scots in a fierce raid in 1327. The abbey itself did not suffer initially as mist had obscured the buildings from the insurgents. Naively, however, the monks immediately tolled the abbey bells to signal that now all was safe. This alerted the raiders to the presence of the abbey; they immediately returned and ransacked it.

The former plan of the abbey can be reasonably discerned as one walks through the village. What is now the parish church of St Mary is partially based on the abbey church. The Crewe trustees found the church in ruins and proceeded to put together an L-shaped space using those walls which were still standing. The monastic crossing, chancel and north transept (at the end of which stands the tower) thus form the church. The chancel is of *c.*1200–1210 and the transept mid thirteenth century, with the strong tower of the same period topped by a fourteenth-century belfry. The chancel aisle was further rebuilt in 1854 and the east end in 1881. In the chancel, there is a much restored, triple sedilia. In the late nineteenth century, a carved and panelled ceiling was added to the chancel.

Moving out of the church, the wall bounding the adjacent inn, the Lord Crewe Arms, is part of the south wall of what was a long and narrow monastic nave. One corbel from the cloister roof survives in the garden of the inn. The inn itself is a remodelling of the west range of the monastic buildings and the other fifteenth-century embattled tower was probably the former 'Abbot's Lodge'. The attractive square at the heart of the village appears to be a rebuilding of a former L-shaped court, reached through a fifteenth-century embattled gatehouse. On the east side is Gowland's Cottage, another altered fifteenth-century building, the southern extension of the east cloister range. The 1897 pant (drinking water fountain) at the centre of the square commemorates Queen Victoria's Diamond Jubilee.

Below: The parish church within the former north transept.

FURNESS ABBEY

n late 2021, a document was discovered relating to the dissolution of Furness Abbey. Within it, Robert Southwell, who had overseen the Dissolution in 1537, describes in detail the process, thus offering great insights into the wider pattern of Dissolution of the Monasteries. He shows, for example, how so many of the artefacts which were of considerable value, including the altar silver, were disposed of and sold locally. Furness was the first of England's greater monasteries to be dissolved.

The origins of the abbey lie in the migration of a colony of monks from Savigny near Avranches in Normandy to Furness in 1124. Along with all other Savignac monasteries it later became a Cistercian foundation, following the merging of the two orders in 1148. The importance of Furness increased and eventually it gave birth to new monasteries including Dundrennan and Sweetheart in Galloway in southern Scotland. The Cistercians remodelled Furness in their own image, later in the twelfth century. The surviving ruins offer a fairly clear picture of the growth and development of the community and its buildings.

The setting of the abbey in a beautiful rocky valley among the trees is stunning. The tiny hamlet of Barrow nearby grew much later into the great centre of shipbuilding which we see today. Much survives of the abbey complex, built of an attractive warm red sandstone. The church is of the normal Cistercian plan with a straight-headed chancel and transepts, each of which had an eastern aisle divided into three chapels. The crossing is that of the original Savignac

church, probably heightened when the Cistercians built the chancel. The nave was originally of ten bays, but the building of the immense west tower (which was never completed) intruded into the westernmost bay of the nave. Unusually, the cloister was oblong, although even elsewhere in this volume one does encounter similar examples. One of the masterpieces of Furness is the series of five magnificent Romanesque arches on the eastern cloister walk; they are impressively elaborate with effectively four orders, reducing in size towards each arch's aperture. The lay brothers' range was impressive with a double nave. The vaulted infirmary chapel survives with its broad but shallow rib vaulting. The 1982 visitor centre adds nothing of architectural distinction to the site, sadly.

To the north is the late twelfth-century great gatehouse, although only the lowest courses survive. Again to the north, following the Dissolution, John Preston built his new Manor House, using the remains of the guest house within the new building. The large abbot's house stood further to the east of this. The Manor House became the Abbey Tavern but regrettably the railway company rebuilt it as the Furness Abbey Hotel and linked it with the station. All that remains after the 1950s demolition is the former second class refreshment room! Near to the Abbey Tavern are the former railway platforms. The precinct wall stands on the southern skyline.

Above: The warm sandstone of Furness Abbey.

WHITBY ABBEY

Set high on a cliff above the town, Whitby Abbey was known from early times as the 'beacon on the hill'. Bede mentions it under its ancient Anglo-Saxon name in his *Ecclesiastical History*: Having been Abbess of Hartlepool, Bede notes of St Hilda: '. . . the Abbess acquired a property of ten hides at a place called Streanaeshalch.' Whitby's significance as a spiritual beacon can be traced to the year 657 when St Hilda, the first abbess, set up a double monastery for men and women. Here, in 664, was the setting for the Synod of Whitby, when Irish and Roman traditions met and set a course for the future, under the oversight of King Oswy and the persuasive and powerful personality of Wilfrid. Nothing is now visible of Hilda's monastery, which disappeared in Viking invasions in 867, although in 1920–25 excavations revealed remains of the early monastery which sadly were not left exposed. The original monastery was of the cenobitic type, with community members living in separate houses with only the church and refectory as common meeting places.

It was not until *c.*1078 that the abbey at Whitby was refounded as a Benedictine monastery, when Reinfrid, a monk from the abbey at Evesham in the West Midlands, made the pilgrimage north. In the years that followed, a Benedictine church was constructed, following the traditional Cluniac pattern with an apsidal chancel, apsidal-ended chancel aisles, and transepts with apsidal chapels.

The view which is most famous today is of the Early English east end which dates from the rebuilding that began in the 1220s. It has three tiers of lancets and these comprise a fairly typical north country elevation. Unusually for England at this time, there is dogtoothing round the windows. The aisled presbytery was built on a grand scale under the direction of Abbot Roger. The rebuilding included the choir with its splendid triforium resting upon Gothic arcades. The completion of this rebuilding had to wait until the fifteenth century with the construction of the great Perpendicular east window. The south transept collapsed in 1763 leaving just one pier. The nave had collapsed a year earlier and the piers at the crossing are little more than short stumps. There are three arches standing dramatically to the north of the church – these are re-erected nave arches.

Virtually nothing of the monastic buildings survives, but to the south of the church lies a grouping of impressive buildings now known as Abbey House, which are thought to stand on the site of the prior's kitchen. The house was originally built for Sir Francis Cholmeley from 1583–1593 and added to with a banqueting hall by his later relative Sir Hugh, between 1672 and1682. This complex has now been converted into the excellent English Heritage Visitor Centre.

The medieval prominence of the abbey is obvious in the scale of the ruined church. The cult of its many saints flourished during the pre-Reformation period and it was this that enabled the community to rebuild the church on such a magnificent scale.

Below: Viewed from the south-east.

RIEVAULX ABBEY

Of the ruined abbeys and priories of England, alongside Fountains Abbey, Rievaulx must be in one of the most stunning locations of all. It was a Cistercian foundation and one of the sixty-four abbeys of that order established in England. The order began in Cîteaux, in 1078, in eastern France, established by St Stephen Harding. It was the result of a reform movement within Benedictinism leading to a stricter rule. Its houses were often built in wild and remote country and the buildings themselves, while often being of substantial size, were austere in their beauty. Their abbeys would include priests and lay brothers – the naves of their churches would be the main territory of the lay brothers who also served the priests within the community. Cistercian abbeys would invariably be built alongside fast-flowing streams supplying good fresh water and a proper means of drainage.

It was Walter Espec, Lord of Helmsley, who brought a colony of Cistercian monks to establish their noble abbey in the narrow valley of the River Rye in 1132. Rievaulx was to become one of the most important Cistercian foundations in England and a great mission centre for the order. In 1147, the Northumbrian, Aelred, became abbot. Aelred was a theologian, who wrote about the monastic life and was an able administrator.

Rievaulx's great church was built in two periods: during the 1150s and then during the 1220s, in the Burgundian Romanesque style. The nave is of nine bays, although sadly little survives; there were screens to the aisles and the aisles themselves were tunnel-vaulted; the west wall of the nave indicates the presence of a large western doorway with buttresses of a wall to the inside leading to a smaller Norman door – there had also been a galilee. Originally, as noted above, the nave was for the lay brothers, with the early thirteenth-century presbytery of seven bays for the monks. The eastern wall of the presbytery has two tiers with three tall lancets on the ground level, three stepped lancets at the next stage and finally two blank trefoils. The high altar's position is marked, two bays from the east end and some eastern tiling is

exposed. In the transepts we encounter richly decorated windows, using nailhead. In the north transept, the north and south walls include three tall upper lancets with just two lancets in the west. In the south transept, which was built later, there are only two lancets. The aisles were rib-vaulted in both transepts.

The monastic ruins are very noble indeed and the pattern is easy to follow. The buildings include a fine corner of the cloister arcade and, in the east range, are the foundations of the very capacious apsidal chapter house; a thirteenth-century shrine of William, the first abbot, obscures one of the openings. The next-door room was the parlatorium which is effectively a passage, and the day staircase to the dormitory followed. Finally, came the treasury and warming house. The dormitory sat above the entire east range. Evidence of the library and vestry survive and above the vestry would have been the sacristy. Of the small west range little survives, although here were housed the armies of lay brothers. The south range was more complex. Here, as was often the case in most monastic houses, lay the refectory, but in this case running north–south and not parallel with the cloister walk. To both the left and right of this range are shafts which would have supported the lavatorium, where monks washed their hands before entering the refectory. To the east of the refectory, were the warming house, the kitchen and the novices' quarters. At the south-east corner lay the infirmary. The south range included the reredorter offering ample lavatory facilities. The abbot's lodging was eventually more than commodious as with similar buildings in medieval abbeys and priories. The infirmary was taken over to provide this extra space.

Finally, of the outer buildings, the Capella Extra Portas (chapel outside the gates) survives and is now the church of St Mary, having been restored by Temple Moore in 1906. There is also some thirteenth-century work, to which Temple Moore added a chancel and tiny steeple.

Rievaulx's position is uniquely beautiful, and the substantial ruins allow one to piece together the daily life of this, the greatest English Cistercian centre of its day.

Rievaulx Terrace, immediately above the abbey, but not part of it, is really part of the landscaping of Duncombe Park. There are two temples, one Ionic and the other Doric.

Below: The monastic ruins viewed from the north-east.

LANERCOST PRIORY

Standing very close to the Scottish border, Lanercost has had an exciting history. Indeed, some of the stone used to build the priory came from Hadrian's Wall, which at nearby Hare Hill survives to its highest level, some seventeen courses of stone. There is a Roman inscription telling of the presence of one Legio VI Victrix now built into the priory wall. It survives, remarkably well preserved, standing peacefully by the River Irthing.

The founder was Robert de Vaux, whose father, Hubert, had recently wrested nearby Gilsland from the Scots – Gilsland is still divided, now between Cumbria and Northumberland. The foundation date of the Augustinian monastery was 1169 and building seems to have started soon after c.1175–80 with the cloister and that part of the church nearest to it. A stumpy cross may mark signs of an earlier start on an aisleless church. The stunning west front with a very rich portal, and the figure of the Magdalen high up near the gable, suggest a completion date of c.1214. The church is cruciform with a square west end but made more complex with a chapel on either side at the intersection of the chancel and transepts. The nave has only a north aisle as in Hexham and Brinkburn. The style is Early English with some Transitional features – there is a good feeling of integrity to the building. Remarkably preserved, it is only the roofs of the eastern end of the church which are missing.

So, from the interior, the chancel and transepts are a controlled ruin in the care of English Heritage.

One can still appreciate fairly clearly the main structure and style of the building. Entering the nave, we see three bays of arcading, separated from a further eastern bay. A good clerestory, with a wall passage on the south side, faces the unaisled north side which is blank. There is some good Morris and Co. glass by Burne-Jones in the north aisle, and memorials to the Dacre family and to the Howard family (of the Earldom of Carlisle) from nearby Naworth Castle. Part of a cross shaft in the blocked north doorway carries an interesting inscription, beginning, 'In the 1,214th year of the incarnation . . . Otto being Emperor of Germany . . .'

The monastic buildings and cloister have been exposed and the western range is still in use. Here was the scriptorium and here now is the Dacre Hall used by the parish, and then the ruinous Dacre Tower. The south range rebuilt c.1250 is partially extant with its vaulted undercroft, but the upper level has been lost. The vicarage is on the site of the old priory farm. The mid thirteenth-century gatehouse survives only in its inner arch with a length of the precinct wall still standing to the north along by the road.

Excitement continued with the wars with Scotland and Edward I lay mortally sick here for five months in 1306–7. In 1312, Robert Bruce made the priory his headquarters inflicting significant damage. Periodic spells of conflict continued into the late fourteenth century.

Above: Lanercost Priory showing the rebuilt parish church.

MONK BRETTON PRIORY

C aught up into the decaying industry of north Barnsley and almost submerged in housing in the suburb of Lundwood, one comes upon this gem. The priory, which began as a Cluniac foundation of St Mary Magdalene of Lund (Lund is from the Old Norse) in 1154, was a daughter house of St John's Priory in Pontefract, established by Adam Fitzwane. As with so many medieval monasteries, the founder had sufficient ingenuity to place their house close to a river or stream to allow for good drainage. Monk Bretton lies on the hilly bank of the River Dearne. Just over a century later in 1281, the monastery seceded from the Cluniac order to become an independent Benedictine house.

Despite its proximity to former coal mining and heavy industry, significant remains have survived. On approach, there is, first of all, the substantial and noble fifteenth-century gatehouse, which sits on earlier foundations. There is a porter's lodge to the west and a large room to the east. Further east still is the large administrative building (*c.*1300) with a double gable and parallel roofs. At the ground floor level there are three monolithic octagonal piers and the upper room has seventeen windows!

The other impressive survival is of the west range of the cloister, which is not far from complete. Here was the prior's lodging. The early thirteenth century included a small outer parlour set over a vaulted cellar and a well. Above this in the mid fourteenth century there was created for the prior a fine upper hall with its own galleried lobby and a splendid chamber fireplace. These apartments were extended further in the fifteenth century. After the Dissolution they became a residence for Edward Talbot, son of the 6th Earl of Shrewsbury, and in the late sixteenth and early seventeenth centuries further rebuilding adapted the lodgings for Talbot's daughter Lady Armyne. Part of the gatehouse built then survives in the form of a timber-framed east wall.

Although the church is largely lost, its basic plan and that of the rest of the monastic buildings, remain very clearly. The church was cruciform with a Cistercian plan with an aisled nave. The late twelfth-century northern arcade was taken and rebuilt within Wentworth church. The thirteenth-century cloister had open arcades. The pattern of the drains is particularly visible, including an ashlar drain to the reredorter with the bottom of the chute from the western latrine intact. South of the reredorter was the guest house and to the east the isolated infirmary. On the south side of the cloister in the traditional place was the refectory – two tall window lights survive and also traces of the lavatorium.

These substantial remains, of some considerable beauty, are a rich asset to the urban centre of Barnsley, both for education and for leisure; a local amenity and educational group continue to do good work here.

Below: The ruins of Monk Bretton Priory.

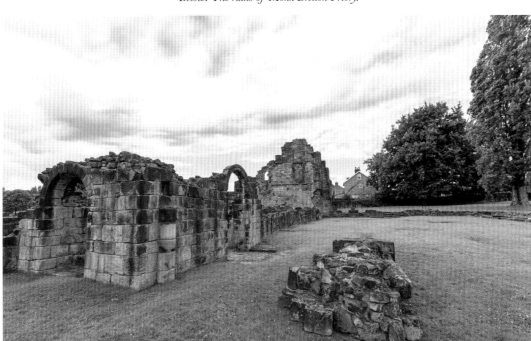

MOUNT GRACE PRIORY

To visit Mount Grace is to encounter a unique expression of the religious life quite distinct from the community pattern seen in Benedictine and Cistercian monasteries. The community was established by the Carthusian order, named after the Chartreuse Mountains in the foothills of the French Alps, where St Bruno established his community in 1084. The characteristically green liqueur takes its name from the same place, where the monks continue to produce the liqueur. In England, through a corruption of the name, Carthusian monasteries are generally known as 'Charterhouses'. Mount Grace is one of only two such medieval monasteries in England, where substantial remains have survived. The other Carthusian foundation of which there are some surviving remains is the Charterhouse in the City of London, where one cloister walk has survived alongside other fragments of the medieval monastery; Charterhouse School takes its name from those buildings, where it was first established following the Dissolution of the Monasteries.

At Mount Grace, one enters the great cloister within which all the monks lived through a gatehouse with a gateway of two bays. In living the Carthusian life, the monks effectively lived as hermits, living within their own cell/domicile in the form of a two-storey dwelling which included space for a small parlour and living room/bedroom, an oratory and facilities for washing and lavatory (the best-preserved lavatory is in the cell immediately to the left of the cell which has been restored). Above was space for

Below: The tower of Mount Grace Priory.

a work room for the monk. One can also see the hatches through which the food for the monks was passed into the dwelling. There was a herb garden next to each cell which was tended by the occupant. The dwellings were set around the great cloister, far larger than in other monasteries, and the small lesser cloister. The layout of these unusual communities is still clearly discernible from the ruins.

All this meant that, of course, on account of the space available, at no time did Mount Grace have many monks. Very instructively, Lowthian Bell, the owner, in 1901, rebuilt one of the cells. English Heritage, who now administer this site on behalf of the National Trust, have further added interpretation to one of the dwellings, giving the visitor a very clear understanding of that part of a Carthusian monk's life. The monks come together only for the nocturnal liturgical hours and, also on Sundays and feast days in the monastic church. The other hours are sung by each monk, separately in his cell. The monks live a rule of silence except for the singing of the liturgy and conversation on what are described as 'grave' subjects. Their diet is strictly vegetarian.

Mount Grace was founded in 1398 by Thomas of Holland, the Duke of Surrey, and was the last but one of the seven charterhouses of England to be founded. The priory sits attractively, beneath the woodland, at the foot of the scarp of the North York Moors. The first aisleless church was constructed from 1398 onwards. The west wall of the church survives with its doorway and window above. There is a chapel to the west of the nave. The tower which is a landmark from the main road is oblong, standing on two 'cross walls'. The chapter house was to the immediate north of the chancel, and the prior lived in rooms to the north west of the nave, with his oriel window allowing him a view over the great cloister. A refectory used only on a limited number of feast days lay to the west. The cloister itself is irregular in shape and approximately 90 by 75 metres (300 by 245 feet) – the church itself is only 27 metres (88 feet) long. In the 1420s the priory had been expanded, the church enlarged, and the tower built. The chapter house had also been completed, along with the rebuilding of other monastic buildings. The house to the east of the chancel of the church and chapter house is thought to be that of the sacrist. There is a lesser cloister which had space for six monks only contrasting with the great cloister which housed seventeen.

Following the Dissolution, the ruins of the priory's great houses were incorporated into two later houses, the first built into a 1654 manor house, thus built rather unusually during the Cromwellian Commonwealth period by Thomas Lascelles. Much

Above: The reconstructed Carthusian monk's cell.

later on, at the turn of the twentieth century, the house was completely remodelled in the style of the Arts and Crafts Movement by the ironmaster, Sir Isaac Lowthian Bell. The dwellings were built on two floors, the living quarters on the ground floor and the workroom on the first floor.

There is a good museum and presentation on the site telling the story of the priory and the later house, which can also be visited.

FOUNTAINS ABBEY

I n 1986, Fountains Abbey and Studley Royal, within which estate it now stands, was declared a World Heritage Site by UNESCO. That gives the setting for this remarkable ruin which, along with Rievaulx, also in Yorkshire, is one of the two most outstanding Cistercian abbeys of England. Some background to the Cistercian order, which eventually established sixty-four abbeys in England alone, is given under the Rievaulx Abbey entry (see page 20). Established in the quiet valley of the Skell in 1132, Abbot Richard founded what was to become one of the greatest monastic foundations in twelfth-century England. Even these ruinous buildings that remain capture the sheer scale of this vast monastery. The Cistercian life was an example of reformed Benedictinism, pioneered in Burgundy in the early twelfth century under the leadership of St Stephen Harding at Citeaux and then by St Bernard at Clairvaux. It was a rule rooted in poverty, simplicity of life and isolation; the intention was to achieve self-sufficiency, to avoid dependence on the

worldliness of medieval society. Fountains Abbey, both in its location and its agricultural base, exemplified this well and it grew so rapidly that brothers were sent off to colonise new abbeys, five of which were in Yorkshire and nearby Lincolnshire.

After the sixteenth-century Dissolution of the Monasteries, the abbey was sold into private ownership to one William Aislabie, then the owner of the adjacent estate of Studley Royal. Its final owner, in the twentieth century, Commander Clare George Vyner, is interesting in himself, inasmuch as he set up the Settlers Society in the 1930s, which aimed to help the unemployed and which established a settlement, for example, in Swarland near Alnwick in Northumberland, to retrain those who had lost their jobs in the Tyneside shipyards. It was Vyner who gifted the abbey and the adjacent Studley Royal estate to the then Department of the Environment. It was subsequently transferred into the hands of English Heritage, who remain the owners, although it is administered by the National Trust.

To understand these ruins fully it is important to realise that the Cistercian life depended on vast numbers of lay brothers who helped run the farms. There were probably 600 lay brothers and up to 120 monks. The great church had its origins in a smaller stone building completed between 1136–50, with the monastic buildings coming slightly later, in 1140. In 1146, however, the church was sacked and burnt by followers of the new Archbishop of York, William Fitzherbert, in a dispute with the then abbot, and the church was not immediately rebuilt, but simply repaired. The next church was begun after the election of the new abbot, Richard of Clairvaux. From 1154–1203 the abbey church was enlarged to accommodate the army of lay brothers, and the new eastern arm of the church was begun in 1203 and completed in the 1220s. Thereafter there was no significant building until Abbot Darnton restored the church *c.*1500 and Abbot Huby built his great north tower, in the period immediately before the Dissolution in 1539.

The style was probably prompted by Abbot Aelred's church at Rievaulx, which had been established *c.*1140. As with Rievaulx, then, it conforms to the Bernardine plan, as at Clairvaux in Burgundy. Thus, it begins as Romanesque with a gradual transition towards the pointed arches of later

Left: The undercroft.

Above: The church and sixteenth-century tower.

Gothic. The eleven-bay nave is monumental in scale; it was not vaulted but had a wagon roof. The new presbytery comprised five bays and was completed *c.*1220, and a Chapel of Nine Altars – a pattern copied a few years later in Durham Cathedral – was built in the following decade. The transepts follow a similar style to that at Rievaulx. Abbot Huby's tower, completed *c.*1500, rises to some 40 metres (130 feet) and points to how the earlier Cistercian ban on bell towers had now fallen away. Despite the scale, the architecture still breathes Cistercian austerity with a restrained clerestory and no triforium.

The monastic buildings reflect both the size of the monastery and demonstrate the pattern of the Cistercian life that it sustained. The chapter house is one of the largest in England and the accommodation for the lay brothers is remarkably vast, the western range which accommodates the lay brothers is some 90 metres (300 feet) long and is the largest of its kind; within this complex too, is the fine vaulting of the cellar and lay brothers' refectory. This range also includes an outer parlour, the cellarium, a latrine block and the infirmary. East of the eastern range lies the abbot's house, the magnificent priests' infirmary and a rather diminutive infirmary chapel. To the west is the site of the fifteenth-century misericord, not on this occasion a 'mercy-seat' for worship, but instead a further hall, where, on occasion, meat could be eaten. These magnificent ruins bear testimony to the crucial influence of the Cistercian life on medieval English society. The Cistercians were pioneers on mining and industry. In 2021, the foundations of a tannery were discovered.

Next door to the abbey is the eighteenth-century landscaped park of the now lost house of Studley Royal, to which estate we have referred earlier.

ROCHE ABBEY

Set stunningly in a glen by Maltby Dyke, Roche was founded by Richard de Busli and Richard FitzTurgis, in 1147. A daughter house of Newminster at Morpeth in Northumberland, the Cistercian plan of the monastery remains very clear. The church survives to a greater height than the other monastic buildings, with the transepts almost at full height. The chancel was of two bays and the nave of eight. Building began *c.*1170 and was complete by the early thirteenth century. Roche was the first Cistercian church in England to have a three-storey elevation.

The monastic buildings grouped around the cloister follow the normal Cistercian plan. The cloister arcade had pointed arches, and the eastern range included the library, sacristy, parlour, day-room and chapter house. The south range was for the refectory, kitchen and warming house. The western range housed the lay brothers, their refectory in the southern half and the dormitory above. In the south-east corner was an irregular secondary cloister

with part of the infirmary and the abbot's lodging. Roche has the most complete surviving gatehouse which greets the visitor on arrival. It is vaulted with an inner court. A vivid account of Roche's sacking at the Dissolution was written in 1591. The site was landscaped by Capability Brown in 1774–77 as part of Sandbeck Park.

Above: The ruins sit in a beautifully designed landscape.

JERVAULX ABBEY

There is a charmingly gentle feel to Jervaulx, made so by its individuality of style and the Burdon family's care for the site. There is a wide variety of wild flowers in the grounds.

Originally a Savigniac abbey, it became Cistercian when the orders merged. Starting at Fors near Aysgarth in 1145, it moved to Jervaulx in 1156. Little of the church survives, save evidence of the two west doorways. With vaulted aisles, it was 90 metres (300 feet) long and built in the late twelfth and early thirteenth centuries.

The cloister, in the traditional southern location, now forms a walled garden. The earliest surviving fabric is in the west range, including the cellar, with the lay brothers' accommodation above. At the west end of this range is the reredorter and then the lay brothers' infirmary. The south range contained the refectory with the kitchen and warming house. In the east range were the chapter house and parlatorium. The dormitory was above and its surviving wall is the great feature at Jervaulx with nine high lancet windows. To the south-west was the misericord, where meat could be eaten. The monks' reredorter and infirmary were located near to the abbot's chapel and hall. Wensleydale cheese was first made here – Jervaulx is a must if it is anywhere near to your itinerary.

Left: The surviving wall of the dormitory, with its high windows, is clearly visible.

SELBY ABBEY

Selby sits on the edge of the east Yorkshire plain, on the River Ouse, just on the edge of the former coalfield. In the 1980s, the area north east of the town hosted a late developing coalfield for a brief spell. The town itself is largely eighteenth- and nineteenth-century with a broad main street, but it remains an unlikely location for the splendid abbey standing towards the north of the town centre and surviving, despite the Dissolution of the Monasteries, largely as it was built.

The abbey is built on slightly raised land in a low-lying area prone to flooding; it thus stands out as a beacon from afar. Legend suggests that a monk of the abbey of St Germain at Auxerre was bidden by a vision of the saint to come to England bringing a relic of Germain's finger with him! William I's foundation charter, of 1070, more certainly sees the first abbey, a wooden structure, being begun by Abbot Benedict; Benedict was later forced to resign and his successor, Hugh, began building the present stone church around 1100. Elements of this Romanesque building still remain. Hugh's vision took more than 130 years to complete and styles changed during the period of building. The abbey was established as a Benedictine foundation, but the monastic buildings disappeared at the Reformation.

Approaching from the west, the abbey is entered by walking beneath the splendid Romanesque carving around the west door, and much of the lower west front dates from this period. On entering the nave, the dominant style is again Romanesque with fine pillars decorated in the same fashion as those in Durham Cathedral. The earliest Romanesque work, and the oldest part of the abbey, is the west wall of the north transept – the north porch is also from the Norman period. By the beginning of the thirteenth century Early English patterns began to predominate and this is clear in the south nave triforium and in the upper levels of the west front. Much of the crossing has been renewed more than once, due to two disasters. The tower collapsed in 1690, doing damage to the south transept and effectively destroying the adjoining chapter house. In 1906, following a fire, the choir roof collapsed and much of the crossing, transepts and nave had to be restored.

The Decorated choir dates from 1280, and this reconstruction concluded with the addition of the fine Jesse window around 1330. In contrast with the flat wooden roof of the nave, the choir roof is a wooden vault with some fine gold bosses. The noble sedilia is thought to be by Henry Yevele, the king's mason, who built the nave of Canterbury Cathedral. The final stages of the western towers (probably intended by the Norman builders) were not completed until 1935, but they give an added dignity to the west front. The abbey has been painstakingly restored in recent years.

Below: The west front.

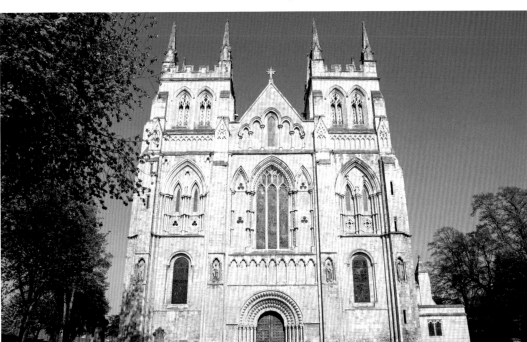

THE KINGDOM OF MERCIA

The mighty Penda was one of the legendary figures in the kingdom of Mercia. He defeated Edwin of Northumbria in 633, then Oswald at Maserfield (modern day Oswestry) in 642 and was himself finally defeated at Winwaed in 655, by Oswald's brother and successor, Oswy. Oswy would preside over the Synod of Whitby in 664, which among other things, would bring together the Irish and Roman monastic traditions, represented by Aidan and Wilfrid respectively. Of the early Irish tradition, it was Chad who became the key figure in Mercia, having first been a bishop in Northumbria and then later in both Lindsey and Mercia. His shrine was in Lichfield and recently a powerful sculpture of the saint has been dedicated outside Lichfield Cathedral. The fact that for a short time there was an Archbishop in Lichfield speaks of the prominence of the Mercian Kingdom. In Lindsey, that is modern Lincolnshire, the twelfth century saw the building of a vast scattering of religious houses. Sadly, there is little evidence above ground of this extraordinary flowering of the monastic tradition. The frontiers of Mercia waxed and waned with the fortunes of the various kings and therefore those boundaries have been drawn generously here.

HAUGHMOND ABBEY

Set on Haughmond Hill, just four miles east-north-east of Shrewsbury, the abbey affords a panoramic view over the Severn valley and the town itself. Even now, though ruinous, you can see that this was a wealthy foundation with a spacious cloister and substantial buildings. The community's beginnings are early twelfth-century and shrouded in some mystery, and a small late Saxon church was unearthed here in excavations in the mid 1970s. There were connections too with Prior Fulk, the Latin Patriarch of Jerusalem in the mid twelfth century. The present abbey for Augustinian canons can be traced back to *c.*1135, when it was re-endowed by Willam Fitzalan, whose family continued to be generous patrons over the following centuries. As noted, the buildings speak of prosperity. The sandstone for the buildings came from the abbey's own quarries at nearby Grinshill. The buildings were sold to Sir Rowland Hill, Lord Mayor of London in 1549, and most of the buildings including the church were demolished. The abbot's lodgings were converted into a family home. This explains the nature of the site today.

The archway into the site is thus Elizabethan/ Jacobean and the front of the stately mansion survives virtually intact, with the features of the front of the abbot's lodgings apparently unaltered. Only the foundations of the church have survived, but this allows one to see the plan and also to gradually ascend the incline on which the church was built – the impact on the interior of the building through this ascent will have been dramatic – indeed the eastern end of the church was cut into the solid rock of the hill. The building was cruciform with a square end to the chancel – it is likely that there was a crossing tower.

Although the main church was completed by the end of the twelfth century, a north aisle and porch were added in the thirteenth century. The church was of significant proportions, 62 metres (200 feet) long. The cloister was to the south of the nave and the splendid triple-arched facade of the chapter house has survived. Transitional in style, there are four orders with rich moulding and eight fourteenth-century figures of saints; the original plan for the chapter house was rectangular. The west range includes an unusually monumental lavatorium. The south range housed the refectory of which some windows survive; the kitchen adjoined to the south.

There was a trapezoidal south cloister bounded to the east by the dormitory range. The ruins of the abbot's lodgings remain very fine, with an early fourteenth-century hall, the detail and ornamentation of which is still distinguished even though now ruinous. The fireplace and chimney breast are post-medieval, added when it became a family home.

Opposite: Hailes Abbey.
Below: Haughmond Abbey viewed from the west.

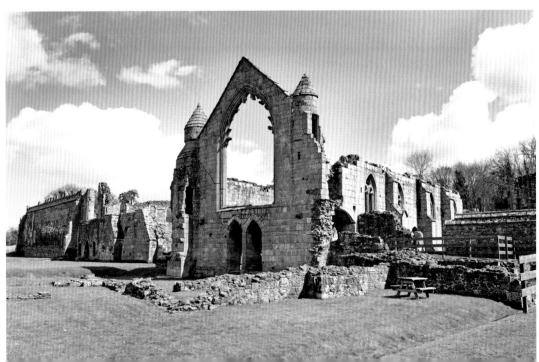

Left: The refectory wall.

went to build the great house there, and there is only scant evidence of Barlings alongside a farm.

Tupholme's refectory wall then is almost symbolic of this heroic past. It was a Premonstratensian abbey founded *c.*1160, and the fragments which survive date from the early thirteenth century. Alongside the earthworks of the cloister and church is the south wall of the refectory, again, dating from the first half of the thirteenth century. It has high lancet windows with five of them being preserved. The reader's pulpit, a stunning piece, is there – recessed into the wall in two bays. To the left of the pulpit is a Norman window. In the wall of the farmyard are stones from ribs similar to those at Bardney Abbey. It appears that somehow Tupholme was connected by a watercourse with the River Witham which runs about one and a half miles away.

Although fragmentary, the remains of Tupholme Abbey are now sadly one of the most significant survivals of medieval religious life in the county, which had more monastic foundations than any other English county. Some of the abbeys were important foundations. These included Revesby, Kirkstead, Barlings and Bardney, where the mortal remains of St Oswald of Northumbria were interred before being exhumed and moved once again. Bardney really only exists as humps but is worth a visit. Much of Revesby

TUPHOLME ABBEY

ABBEY DORE

Abbey Dore lies in the beautiful Golden Valley, only a short distance from the Welsh border – its name is taken from the river and the former abbey. Here is one of only two Cistercian abbey churches in England still used as a parish church. Dore Abbey was founded in 1147, by Robert de Ewyas with monks from Morimond Abbey in the Champagne-Ardenne region of eastern France. The abbey, with its cruciform church, including a chancel of only two bays, was built between *c.*1175 and 1220. Only fifty years later, in the thirteenth century, the chancel was extended. None of the other conventual buildings survive except for a tiny remnant of the chapter house and slight traces of the north range.

This means that the present building, which is of 'village church proportions', has a certain quirkiness to it. That is partly on account of the fact that the complete nave of the abbey church is entirely gone. The transepts and crossing survive, with clear late Norman features, and with a chancel of three

bays. The present Laudian style of the interior and furnishings owe much to the beneficence of the first Lord Scudamore, who restored the building *c.*1632–33, adding the tower with its lancets and battlements; the church was reconsecrated in 1635.

Above: Abbey Dore has been restored as a parish church.

WENLOCK PRIORY

Here we find ourselves in the former kingdom of Mercia and on the edge of the Welsh Marches in the beautiful and ancient town of Much Wenlock. The site of the priory is perhaps the most ancient remnant of all in the town, as the site of the earliest monastery, from which the town grew. The first foundation here was by Merewald, King of Mercia, but even then, using a former Roman building. Apparently, a double monastery, it was the demesne of the king's daughter Milburga, who was the first abbess. Double monasteries required two churches for priests and for sisters – the first is the site of the surviving remnants of the abbey church and the other was on the site of what is now Holy Trinity parish church.

In 1050 the priory was generously endowed by Leofric, Earl of Mercia and a confidant of Edward the Confessor. In c.1079–82, a Cluniac monastery was established by Roger de Montgomery, a generous benefactor of the Abbey at Cluny. Monks were brought over from a Cluniac daughter house in the Loire valley. The surviving church ruins are of the church rebuilt in the early years of the thirteenth century, although some Romanesque fragments remain, as indeed does the fine prior's lodging of the fifteenth century.

The nave was eight bays in length and originally had drum-shaped piers. The later piers followed the design of the transept piers with a number of shafts, but sadly these are largely lost. Three storeys of the transepts survive, and the lower courses of the crossing remain. In the transepts there are tall triforia and waterleaf pattern on the pier capitals. The presbytery also had drum-shaped piers and there was a processional route in the eastern bay to the shrine of St Milburga. The west front had a central portal of five shafted orders and then a substantial north porch, the foundations of which survive – this was doubtless to accommodate pilgrims entering on their way to St Milburga's shrine. The Lady Chapel was a later addition further to the east in the early fourteenth century. The church was undoubtedly the largest monastic church in the county, approximately 117 metres (380 feet) in length.

Of the conventual buildings, the cloister walks have vanished but the surrounding buildings yield much of interest. The free-standing lavatorium, whose remains survive, was unique in England. The library is at the north-east corner and next adjoining the south transept is the chapter house. There are remains of the dormitory range, but these are not publicly accessible. The rererdorter was further to the south. The refectory was to the south of the cloister with the lavatorium in the south-west corner of the cloister. The fifteenth-century prior's lodging and infirmary were rebuilt, after the Dissolution, into the adjacent private house known as Wenlock Abbey. The prior's hall is a magnificent room with an open timber roof of c.1425. Little survives of the refectory. Much Wenlock exists on account of the priory. It is a lovely town and worth further exploration.

Above: Looking towards the entrance to the cloister.

TEWKESBURY ABBEY

Putting on one side the great cathedrals of Durham, Norwich and Winchester, the Abbey Church of St Mary the Virgin, Tewkesbury is the single most important example of Romanesque architecture in England. The nave arcading with its immense drum-like piers is remarkable and the crossing tower is the largest Romanesque crossing tower in Europe. Entering the building induces an immediate sense of awe at the sheer scale and power of this vast transcendent space.

Tradition suggests that a Saxon Benedictine monastery was founded at Tewkesbury in the early part of the eighth century. The likelihood is then that there was a Saxon minster church here from *c.*980. The present building dates from the Norman refoundation by Robert Fitzhamon in 1087. In 1102, monks moved here from Cranborne, indicating that the east end and perhaps the first two bays of the nave had been finished. By the time of Fitzhamon's death in 1107, the church was still incomplete – it was finally consecrated *c.*1121–23. The tower was not finished until the mid twelfth century. The interior of the building in the nave echoes the Norman origins of the church throughout, with its dominant circular columns, which appear to derive from French examples of similar work either in Burgundy or Poitou; the nave is contemporary with the nave of Gloucester Cathedral. The Lady Chapel was a perfect example of a Romanesque apsidal chapel.

The remodelling in the early fourteenth century was almost certainly due to the energy of Hugh le Despenser, who married into the de Clare family, which had inherited the 'Honour of Tewkesbury'. The clerestory, vault and some of the most precious stained glass date from this period. After this, only the Founder's Chapel and Trinity Chapel were added in the late fourteenth century, followed by the Warwick or Beauchamp *c.*1430. The chevet of chapels around the apse, again a strong echo of the French influence, were constructed in the early fourteenth century.

The collection of tombs, chantry chapels and monuments is rivalled in England only by Westminster Abbey. The fine chantry chapels for the Despenser, Fitzhamon and Beauchamp families date from 1390 and 1425. The Despenser chapel is an

Right: The Romanesque nave with its splendid arcading.

Above: The crossing tower.

early example of fan vaulting and includes fragmentary gold-leaf painting on the east wall. The Beauchamp chapel is the latest and most magnificent of the Tewkesbury chantries, again displaying sumptuous vaulting. The monastic buildings were largely to the south of the present church, but these disappeared at the Reformation. Only the abbot's

gateway (c.1500) remains. West of the gateway is part of a timber-framed medieval barn, which may have been the almonry barn; the cottages to the south-west may have been part of the almonry house.

The 'Laborare et Orare' windows by Tom Denny, on the south side, commemorating the monks' arrival from Cranborne, were completed in 2002.

PERSHORE ABBEY

ershore Abbey, sitting in its meadow, is dominated by the splendid tower of *c.*1327 and the massive buttresses of 1913 shoring up the east end. It has an eccentric history. Founded in 689 by King Ethelred of Mercia's nephew, Oswald, and refounded by King Edgar in 972, much of its land was confiscated by Mercian grandees, when the Benedictine rule was introduced in 976. The land was later given by King Edward the Confessor to Westminster Abbey, thus dividing the town between two foundations.

Only the crossing, transepts and presbytery survived the Reformation, but the interior is very fine.

Romanesque arcading survives in the south transept with intersecting arches of chevron and nailhead mouldings which are very fine. The chancel vault of *c.*1288 is among the finest in England and of great historical importance. In 1864 and 1887, Sir Gilbert Scott and Sir Aston Webb successively restored the church in a graceful manner. The interior is stunning, notably the chancel vault. Against the west wall, the two Jacobean and canopied Haselwood monuments are interesting. The layout of the monastic buildings, which included a small cloister, was excavated in 1929–30 but nothing survives above ground. The Norman chapter house was round in plan.

Below: Viewed from the north-west.

Above: The remains of the cloister.

HAILES ABBEY

Here is one of the last of the host of Cistercian abbeys established in England. The importance of the abbey grew remarkably, when in 1270, Edmund, son of Richard, Earl of Cornwall, presented a phial of the Holy Blood to Hailes Abbey, which transformed the monastery into one of the most celebrated pilgrimage centres of medieval England.

Hailes had been founded twenty-five years earlier, by Richard, Earl of Cornwall, through the gift of the manor of Hailes by Henry III, who was Richard's brother. His foundation was by monks from the monastery in Beaulieu in Hampshire. Richard was later crowned 'King of the Romans' as he sought to become Holy Roman Emperor. This led to him setting up a rich endowment to the abbey and there was a grand consecration of the foundation in 1251. By then many of the conventual buildings had been completed according to the normal Cistercian pattern; all was finally ready by *c.*1255. In 1272, Richard was buried alongside his second wife, Sanchia of Provence. The abbey became very well-known and the destination of large numbers of pilgrims. In his *Pardoner's Tale*, Geoffrey Chaucer writes: 'By the blode of Crist that is in Hayles.' The abbey gained in richness through pilgrimage and trade in wool. Some time after the Dissolution, in the seventeenth century, the Tracy family colonised the west range of the cloister, converting it into a family home, but it was ruinous by 1732.

The Cistercian church comprised a four-bay presbytery and an eight-bay nave, the last five bays of which were for the lay brothers. The transepts each had three chapels. The cloister ruins include some fifteenth-century rebuilding, with just some small evidence of the window tracery. Three bays of the inner walls of the fifteenth-century cloister (which had been a square of ten bays) survive at the southern end of the western range, and a substantial part of the east range is visible. The triple arch to the chapter house still stands to full height, otherwise little of the monastic buildings remain, but the pattern of the former monastery is clearly set out for the visitor.

The arrival of the Holy Blood led to the rebuilding of the east end of the presbytery with a corona of chapels (a 'chevet') to house the shrine. There is a good museum, which includes six splendid bosses found in the chapter house; one of these shows Samson breaking the jaws of a lion, thus prefiguring Christ's breaking the doors of death. Alongside these there are also six late fifteenth-century bosses from the east cloister walk.

DORCHESTER ABBEY

The Abbey Church of St Peter and St Paul is one of the early shrines of English Christianity. Dorchester had been a Roman town and was later adopted by the Mercians. The town was given to St Birinus in 634 by Cynegils, King of Wessex and became a missionary centre for the south of England – indeed it was such a centre that its diocese was the largest in England, extending all the way from the Thames to the Humber. The diocese, having moved temporarily to Winchester in 869, thereafter, Dorchester formally became the cathedral church. In 1072, the diocese moved the bishop's seat to Lincoln; even then, it was not until after the Reformation that the diocese became less expansive with the creation of the dioceses of Oxford, Peterborough and Ely. Controversy has continued as to whether Dorchester Abbey should be the cathedral of the diocese of Oxford instead of Christ Church, Oxford.

Dorchester Abbey's origins lie then with the baptism of the pagan king Cynegils by St Birinus in 635. The abbey was refounded as an Arrouaisian Augustinian monastery in 1140; the Arrouaisian order wore a white habit in contrast to the normal black of most Augustinians. The superb abbey church and abbey guest house are still extant.

There is evidence on the north side of Saxon masonry, presumably from the eight-century abbey, which it is believed was complete by 720. As noted, the present building dates from 1140, with the first abbot being one Alured who was still abbot in 1163. The late twelfth-century church was cruciform in plan but without aisles. Some of this work survives on the north side. It is not certain whether the twelfth-century church had a central tower.

In the thirteenth century the church was enlarged with the building of a north choir aisle and a chapel east of the north transept. The sanctuary was remodelled in the Decorated period with fine tracery and glass in the great east window and the unique Tree of Jesse window in the north, while the sedilia anticipate the Perpendicular style with its pinnacled canopies; the Jesse window is one of the jewels of this fine building. In the north choir aisle, there is a beautiful glass roundel depicting the blessing of St Birinus by Archbishop Asterias of Milan, while the south choir aisle houses the Birinus shrine and the famous 'action effigy' of a knight. The chancel stalls with poppyheads were given by Abbot Beauforest in the early sixteenth century. In the seventeenth century half of the north transept was demolished along with the east transept chapel; the western tower was also rebuilt in the seventeenth century. The chancel was restored in the nineteenth century successively by James Cranston, William Butterfield and Gilbert Scott. More recent work has seen the whole church redecorated, the fourteenth-century wall painting in the People's Chapel restored, and a breathtaking display of medieval stonework created in the newly built oak-framed Cloister Gallery.

Above: The tower and nave of Dorchester Abbey.
Opposite: Castle Acre Priory.

EAST ANGLIA

Historically, the origins of the Christian Church in East Anglia are among the most fascinating in England. St Felix, a Burgundian, was sent by the Roman mission in Canterbury to found an East Anglian see. He did this in 633, probably at Felixstowe. Later the see moved to Dunwich, and then to North Elmham, Thetford and finally in 1096 to Norwich. In the mid seventh century, St Fursey brought a Celtic mission from the west coast of Ireland, setting up a monastery within the walls of the abandoned Roman fortress at Burgh Castle, behind Great Yarmouth. Later in the seventh century St Cedd, a Northumbrian Celt, built a stone church – much of which remains – at Bradwell in Essex.

In later medieval times the Benedictine order left its marks. The largest church in East Anglia was the abbey church at Bury St Edmunds, the ruins of which lie near to the present cathedral; at Peterborough, Ely and Binham in north Norfolk, fine monasteries were built. Other orders left their mark – the ruined Cluniac priory at Castle Acre boasts one of the finest Norman facades in England. Generally, East Anglia is a very rich quarry for churches, abbeys and priories – perhaps per square mile, the richest in England.

WALTHAM ABBEY

The small town of Waltham Abbey lies on the very edge of Essex; it precariously preserves its character as a country town, with its identity determined entirely by the Norman abbey, standing on the site of earlier seventh- and eighth-century wooden then stone churches. The abbey, as we see it today, is but a fragment of the original monastic complex, even though it was the last of the monasteries to be dissolved, in 1540, at the end of Thomas Cromwell's purge of the English religious foundations.

The present church has had a fascinating history, beginning in 1066. The church had been consecrated in 1060 by King Harold. Harold Godwinson triumphed at Stamford Bridge, and on his way south to defeat at Hastings made pilgrimage to the Holy Cross, at the abbey at Waltham, which he himself had established. After his defeat he was buried in the abbey, to the west of the high altar. This magnificent shrine to a hapless king remains a gem, just avoiding being caught up in London's northern sprawl. Stunning Romanesque arcading survives, and it was unusually enhanced by an imaginative and inspired Victorian restoration by William Burges. Burges' painted ceiling, prompted by that at Peterborough Cathedral, is a triumph.

Harold founded the church as a minster, staffed by twelve secular canons, in the late 1050s. In 1177 it was enlarged; it became an Augustinian abbey in 1184. The east end marks the former crossing of the church; the crossing tower fell in 1553 bringing down the transepts with it. Burges' east wall above the medieval screen was an entirely new creation and adds much beauty, rooted, as it is, in the thirteenth-century style. The Norman nave is of seven bays. Its columns rank with those at Durham and Norwich, with the alternating composite and plain round piers. The large gallery is characteristic of other great churches in eastern England including Ely and Norwich Cathedrals. The western tower is of 1556–58 using stones from the old crossing tower and incorporating the remains of the fourteenth-century west front. The old nave was separated off to the south by a screen and *c.*1300, a south chapel was added with its own undercroft. This is now the elevated Lady Chapel with its fifteenth-century Doom painting, but it was built originally for the use of the Guild of the Holy Sepulchre. Sir Anthony Denny, into whose possession the abbey fell after the Dissolution, built a family burial chapel, and the Elizabethan Denny Tomb is a delight. Thomas Tallis was organist here in the sixteenth century before he moved on Canterbury Cathedral.

The monastic remains are sparse and include the abbey gatehouse to the north of the west front. North-east of the church is a passage which led north from the north-east corner of the cloister. Excavated remains of the abbey forge and pond are to the north-east, with the late fourteenth-century Stoney Bridge between them.

Below: Viewed from the south-east.

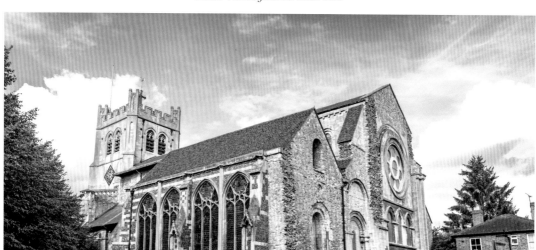

BINHAM PRIORY

Here is one of the glories of Norfolk's monastic treasury, which is, among other places in East Anglia, the subject of a dramatic print by the artist, John Piper. The approach to the priory is through the remains of the fifteenth-century monastic gatehouse. Once through the gateway, the west front of the church is revealed, which is dramatic in itself. Matthew Paris dates the work to before 1244, which makes it the first example of its style in England. There are three doorways with plenty of dogtooth carving to give interest to the portals. The upper windows and their treatment is what adds to the drama of the front. Of the three, only the larger top window survives – the others have been bricked in. It is circular with smaller circular decoration around its perimeter. There is a small bellcote surmounting the front. Binham appears to be also the earliest surviving example of bar tracery in England.

The Benedictine priory was founded as a cell of St Albans Abbey by Peter de Valoines *c.*1091. The remains of the church, including the roofed nave, are extensive. Having now entered through the main portal of the west front, we are greeted by a beautiful and fascinating interior. The nave was built later than the chancel and transepts, and was nine bays long, seven of which now form the parish church. The aisles have been lost but at the north-west corner, Donald Insall Architects have built a small addition on the footprint of the aisle to provide modest facilities including lavatories. The present east wall is the former pulpitum, making clear that the other two bays of the nave formed part of the monastic choir. The two doorways through the pulpitum are original

and the southern door has now been reopened to form an extra door into the churchyard. The nave runs its length at three levels with a gallery and then clerestory with its own narrow wall passage. Architectural evidence suggests that the nave remained unfinished for a considerable period. The font is octagonal, and Perpendicular in style, with the seven sacraments represented beneath the bowl. Four dado panels of the screen survive, attractively painted with extracts from Tyndale's Bible and Coverdale's Psalter, according to Cranmer's version of 1539. Within the nave is some modern artwork, including a brown dossal with an applique 'Christ in Majesty' which has been received ambivalently although acclaimed by some.

There is a good painting by Arthur Hundleby, late churchwarden, of the nave interior with some similarities to the style of Piper. There are benches with traceried backs and poppyheads and two stalls with misericords. The nave has a particularly fine acoustic and is regularly used for concerts.

Outside in the churchyard, the ruins are very considerable. Elements of the east end and crossing and two-bay chancel survive, despite significant demolition in 1540. To the south, the remains of the monastic buildings, now in the care of English Heritage, give a very clear picture of the layout of the priory. The cloister is easily discernible as are the ground plans of the chapter house, dormitory, warming house, refectory and kitchen.

Above: The nave viewed from the south-west.

ST BENET'S ABBEY

Above: The gatehouse and eighteenth-century windmill.

St Benet's is unique for three distinct reasons. First, its position within the flatlands of the River Bure and Norfolk Broads, visible from a distance on account of its second unique feature, the early eighteenth-century windmill (1728–35), built brutally into the otherwise impressive fourteenth-century gatehouse. Finally, St Benet's is the only monastic foundation where the post of abbot survives to this day. The abbey lands were vested in the Bishop of Norwich and the bishop is still Abbot of St Benet's. On the first Sunday in August annually, the bishop presides at the eucharist. The abbey can be visited by road from a turning to the right between Horning and Ludham, or by boat – there is a mooring on the River Bure.

The abbey was founded *c.*800 and later refounded as a Benedictine monastery in 1019. Apart from the mutilated gatehouse little survives. To the east of the gatehouse, are hollows indicating the location of the former fishponds. There are also fragments of the former crenellated enclosing wall in places. Scattered remains of the aisleless church, which had both a western and central tower, survive. There is a wall to the south marking the chapter house and south of this would have run the dormitory with its reredorter (the lavatories), conveniently close to the river.

CASTLE ACRE PRIORY

The impressive ruins at Castle Acre are of a priory of the Cluniac congregation of Benedictine monks. The Cluniac reform aimed to establish a 'congregation' such that each priory was not independent but grouped with others, and thus reform and discipline could be more easy and effective across the order. Originally, all priories would have looked to the 'mother house' at Cluny in Burgundy. Thetford Priory was also part of this congregation, as was Monk Bretton in Yorkshire, before it reverted to the main Benedictine Order. The origins of this priory spring from the period of construction that followed the Norman Conquest, when in 1090 William of Warenne, the second Earl of Surrey, founded the monastery – it

was effectively a daughter house of Lewes priory which had been established as early as 1070. Although there were only twenty-five to thirty monks these buildings are of some grandeur. Indeed, many would argue that these are the most magnificent monastic remains in East Anglia.

Set on the banks of the River Nar, the priory ruins include a fifteenth-century gatehouse to the north, a very noble twelfth-century west front, with the prior's lodgings on its south side, within which there is a small museum and an interactive exhibition. There is considerable evidence of the church and claustral buildings, and the modified remains of the prior's lodging. The presbytery of the church began with an apsidal east end but this was replaced in the

Above: The west front.

early fourteenth century by a larger square ending; the aisles and transepts were groin-vaulted. The west front is in three parts including a main doorway of four orders, with elaborate mouldings, and set within the context of a triple series of blind arcades. Little is visible of the structure of the nave, except for the bay forming the south-west tower.

The monks' dormitory and the reredorter (latrines), together with the refectory (only the walls of which survive) and infirmary, can all be identified. The chapter house adjoined the south transept and originally had a tunnel vault, an apse and more blind arcading. The prior's lodging, with its splendid oriel window, at one time took in the entire western range of the building and is still partially roofed. The north end was divided off to form a parlatorium, which was also tunnel-vaulted, with a chapel above – there are traces of fourteenth-century wall paintings on the window jambs and the east and south walls. The priory gatehouse is of *c.*1500 and of knapped flint, clunch and brick dressings.

Within the village is one of the most impressive motte and bailey castles in England, also established by William of Warenne. The powerful perpendicular parish church was begun in 1396 and makes a visit to this impressive village still more fulfilling.

WALSINGHAM PRIORY

Walsingham remains one of the most magnetic pilgrim destinations in England – there are separate Anglican, Roman Catholic and Orthodox pilgrim centres. The origins of the abbey and the shrine and other pilgrim sites lie in a vision of Our Lady experienced in 1061 by an Anglo-Saxon noblewomann, one Richelde of Fervaques, when she was instructed to build a replica of the house of the Holy Family in Nazareth, in honour of the Annunciation. Her son travelled to the Holy Land in 1095 as part of the First Crusade. On his return he gave land for the establishment of an Augustinian priory with building beginning in 1153. Henry II and Edward I were both supportive. The village which sprang up, Little Walsingham, became almost entirely focused on pilgrimage. Erasmus commented in 1511 that the village was 'maintained by scarcely anything else but the number of its visitors'. That is once again true in modern times.

The most impressive surviving ruin is the fifteenth-century east wall of the church with its east window and two turrets. Sufficient of the north and south walls of the chancel remain to indicate a wall passage beneath the windows. Lady Clare left significant bequests (*a l'overaigne de l'église*) in the mid fourteenth century and there is clear evidence of building between 1360 and 1390. The nave was aisled and, as at St Benet's Abbey, there were two towers at the west end and the crossing – evidence makes it clear that the church was completed towards the end of the thirteenth century.

The refectory was, as normal, to the south of the cloister and its south wall is almost intact. There is no surviving evidence of the west range, but of the east range, three bays of the early fourteenth-century dormitory undercroft remain, and this part is now incorporated into Abbey House. Two corner shafts are all that survive of the chapter house. The shrine, in the chapel of Our Lady, with its image of the seated Virgin, stood to the north of the north aisle.

There were also healing wells to the east of the church, and similarly to the east, was a detached chapel of St Lawrence within which part of a Romanesque doorway has been erected. The gatehouse from the town stands in line with the church and is fifteenth century. The grounds of the priory, as now set out, are attractively presented with a stream running to the east of the church and both wild and manicured gardens.

Elsewhere there is much to be seen in the village, including some remains of a fourteenth-century friary, the Anglican shrine built 1931–37 including some good recent buildings, and the curiously converted former railway station which is now the Orthodox chapel of St Seraphim of Sarov.

Below: The ruins and grounds of Walsingham Priory.

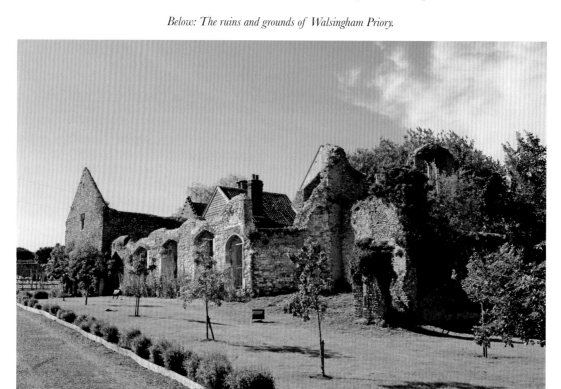

WYMONDHAM ABBEY

Wymondham Abbey cannot be missed as one approaches closer to Norwich on the main London road. Its two towers, to the east and west of the present building dominate the plateau crossed by the main road. They still speak of the strength of the Benedictine abbey founded in 1107, and substantially completed by 1130, and, without a doubt, one of the great conventual churches of England. Happily, the nave has been preserved as the parish church. The town of Wymondham can be traced back to Anglo-Saxon times, but the abbey itself was established in early Norman times by William d'Albini in 1107. It was a Benedictine foundation and a daughter house of St Albans.

The nave retains its Romanesque arcading at the ground floor and triforium levels. The splendid clerestory was remodelled in the mid fifteenth century. This reveals an interesting story of tension between the monks and the people of the town, by whom William d'Albini had also intended the church to be used. In 1249 Pope Innocent IV became involved in the issuing of a papal bull through which the town were given the nave, the north aisle and the north-west tower. The Archbishop of Canterbury became involved in the controversy since Henry IV sent him to adjudicate in 1411. The tension continued and the two towers are both defiant gestures, one by town, one by the abbey! The townspeople were behind the construction of the western tower, which was completed in 1498. Land had been granted for it in 1445, and in 1447 Sir John de Clifton left money for its construction. The north aisle represents the parochial widening of the Norman aisles

The hammerbeam nave roof was constructed during the fifteenth-century remodelling, and the organ case given in 1793. The fine East Anglian octagonal font was moved to its present position in the early twentieth century; against the stem there are depicted four lions and four Wild Men and then against the bowl there are signs for the Evangelists, and angels holding shields. Fragments of a very beautiful thirteenth-century font of Purbeck marble are preserved in a room above the porch. The terracotta sedilia is unusual, the lime wash giving it the appearance of stone. The eastern monastic tower, which formerly crowned the crossing is late fourteenth to early fifteenth century (1390–1509). The magnificent rood, tester and reredos by Sir Ninian Comper were completed with their

Above: The nave and two towers, viewed from the east.

gilding in 1934. The statue of the Virgin and Child in the Lady Chapel is also by Comper (1947).

To the south, in the meadow, some stumps of walls are visible above the ground, helping to give further evidence of the shape and extent of the former conventual buildings. Some of the stonework remains in the churchyard testify to the size of the former choir. Standing by itself to the south is the eastern gable of the chapter house. In 2015, new facilities, designed by Henry Freeland helped to rehabilitate the eastern tower allowing for a visitor centre, shop and other ancillary rooms.

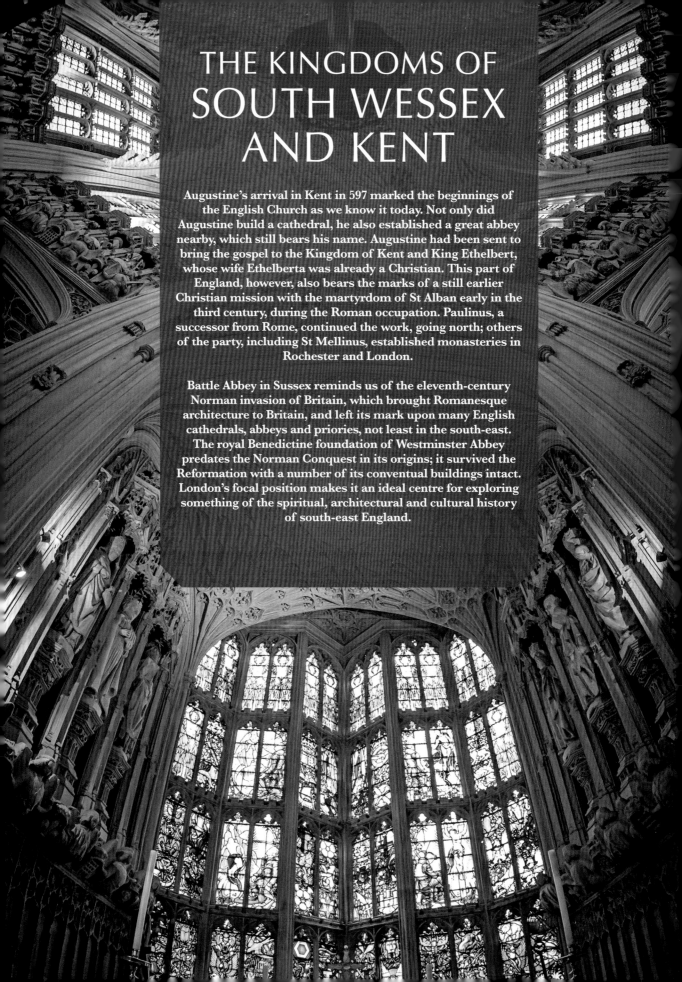

THE KINGDOMS OF SOUTH WESSEX AND KENT

Augustine's arrival in Kent in 597 marked the beginnings of the English Church as we know it today. Not only did Augustine build a cathedral, he also established a great abbey nearby, which still bears his name. Augustine had been sent to bring the gospel to the Kingdom of Kent and King Ethelbert, whose wife Ethelberta was already a Christian. This part of England, however, also bears the marks of a still earlier Christian mission with the martyrdom of St Alban early in the third century, during the Roman occupation. Paulinus, a successor from Rome, continued the work, going north; others of the party, including St Mellinus, established monasteries in Rochester and London.

Battle Abbey in Sussex reminds us of the eleventh-century Norman invasion of Britain, which brought Romanesque architecture to Britain, and left its mark upon many English cathedrals, abbeys and priories, not least in the south-east. The royal Benedictine foundation of Westminster Abbey predates the Norman Conquest in its origins; it survived the Reformation with a number of its conventual buildings intact. London's focal position makes it an ideal centre for exploring something of the spiritual, architectural and cultural history of south-east England.

WESTMINSTER ABBEY

One cannot exaggerate the significance of Westminster Abbey's place in national life. Not only is it the burial place of kings, but also where the monarch is crowned. It is the church for many poignant national occasions and the home of memorials of many who have contributed to the political, scientific and cultural life of the nation. A community of Benedictine monks was first settled here by St Dunstan around 960, but the abbey and collegiate church of Westminster owe much to the refoundation by Edward the Confessor, even though none of his church is now visible above the ground. The abbey was established on Thorney Island, on the banks of what is now called Westminster and when the Thames was still muddy, wide and sluggish. St Edward (as he later became) the Confessor rebuilt the abbey in Romanesque style, completing it in 1065. He died a few weeks later and his shrine remains at the heart of the abbey.

The church as we now know it is largely the work of King Henry III, who began the demolition of the eastern part of the Norman church in 1245 and set about rebuilding in the Early English style. That style is clearly visible in the chancel and the grand plan for the new church was never abandoned, despite the extended period of its rebuilding. The most familiar external views of the abbey are from Parliament Square, which indicate very clearly the strong French influence. It is the most French in style of all English Gothic churches, with its radiating chapels around the apse and ambulatory. Even Henry Yevele, the mason who built the nave (and who also rebuilt the nave of Canterbury Cathedral in its majestic Perpendicular style), continued the plan laid out a hundred years before, when he completed the western part of the nave, beginning in 1375. The unusual height of the nave vaulting – 31 metres (102 feet) – is a further sign of the French influence.

The external niches above the Great West Door are now filled with effigies of ten twentieth-century martyrs, including the Polish monk Maximilian Kolbe. The twin towers are a late addition, designed by Christopher Wren, modified by Nicholas Hawksmoor, and completed by his successor, John James. The western nave was the last part of the medieval building to be completed, in 1403. Immediately inside the west door is the grave of the Unknown Warrior, placed there after the Great War, and a memorial to Sir Winston Churchill.

One moves from the nave into the quire through a screen, to find oneself among stalls completed in 1848. The quire opens into the crossing and the whole of this eastern arm, including the chapter house, was complete by 1259. The chancel is divided by the reredos into the presbytery and the chapel, which encloses the shrine of Edward the Confessor. The pavement around the shrine is thirteenth-century patterned Cosmati work, of similar design to the pavement in the presbytery. The shrine itself still includes the recesses where the sick knelt, hoping for a cure through the relics of the saint. The Coronation Chair of 1301 is nearby; the Stone of Scone which was set beneath the seat is now once again in Scotland, in Edinburgh Castle. Around the shrine runs the ambulatory with its radiating chapels of St John the Baptist, St Paul, St Nicholas, St Edmund and St Thomas.

Above: Looking towards the screen and crossing.
Opposite: Fan vaulting in the Henry VII Chapel,
*   Westminster Abbey.*

Beyond the chancel and the shrine the vista opens up to the dazzling fan vaulting of the Henry VII Chapel; this late Perpendicular masterpiece was completed in 1509. The pendant-like vaulting is stunning. The cloisters were rebuilt after a great fire in 1298, although the eastern walk includes some work from earlier in the thirteenth century. The little cloister with its surrounding houses stands on the site of the monastic infirmary. The splendid chapter house stands on the east side of the east cloister. Dean's Yard was originally partly covered by monastic buildings and the chapter office and school houses incorporate much of the fourteenth-century guest house and cellarers' quarters. Far more of the monastic complex has survived here because of the close links between the abbey and the state.

One cannot begin to catalogue the tombs and memorials which find their place in this remarkable building. Alongside kings, stand memorials to countless literary figures in Poets' Corner; Sir Isaac Newton and other great scientists are remembered in the nave – politicians and soldiers complete the catalogue of the makers of English history.

Most recent of all has been the opening of the Queen's Diamond Jubilee Galleries in the triforium. Designed by Ptolemy Dean, both galleries and means of access are a triumph. The Weston Tower containing the lift nestles in a corner next to the chapter house, adding an elegant external flourish to the medieval fabric. Similarly, the adjacent wooden staircase and fenestration is a model of contemporary design and craftsmanship. The galleries include some 300 remarkable objets – effigies of monarchs, Wren's model of his unrealised tower design and a concertina paper model of the interior of the abbey completed for Queen Victoria's Coronation.

Above: The north porch.
Opposite: The west front.

THE COLLEGIATE CHAPEL OF ST GEORGE AT WINDSOR

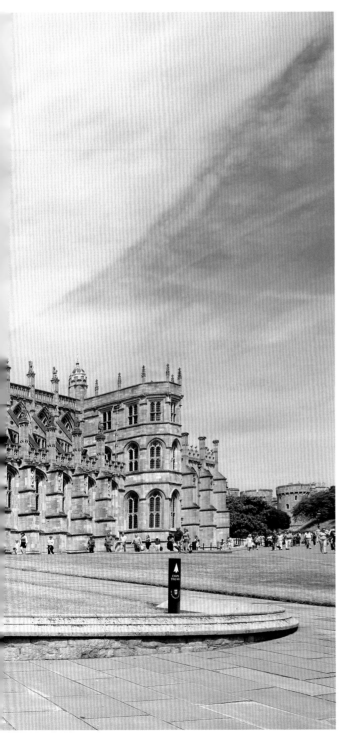

Left: The view from the gatehouse.

Alongside Westminster Abbey, this building is one of the key carriers of the tradition of Church and Monarchy in England and is now the burial place for kings and queens. Although strictly neither a priory nor an abbey, the Chapel of the College of St George is a collegiate church and the cloisters adjoining the chapel breathe a community atmosphere. As the Chapel of the Most Honourable and Noble Order of the Garter, its national significance is further enhanced by the hatchments of the members of the order emblazoned above the stalls. The musical tradition of the chapel is rightly celebrated and St George's House had become something of a 'Staff College' for both Church and State.

The chapel was founded by Edward IV, in 1475, as the royal chapel and for the ceremonies of the Order of the Garter. The Garter ceremonies had previously had as their home Henry III's chapel, which is further to the east. The choir was roofed by 1484 but without a vault. Henry VII warmed to the idea of the new chapel rather slowly but eventually embraced it. The transepts were completed by 1503 and the entire building (save for a crossing tower which was never built) by 1512. The nave is of seven bays and the choir of seven plus an extra eastern bay. The transepts (the Rutland Chantry is effectively a transept) have polygonal and not circular ends. The details are extraordinarily rich and sumptuous but the actual patterns are repetitive. All the evidence suggests that a further western bay was originally intended. Throughout the past five centuries there have been extensive restorations, although the original stone was Taynton, with Reigate and Caen stone internally. Scott's grand wide staircase at the west front was added in 1872.

It is the vault that is the crowning glory of the chapel – the design of this late Perpendicular vaulting is complex, intricate and yet supremely elegant. In the aisles we find fan vaulting which was a remarkable innovation for the date of building. The crossing has the one major fan vault in the chapel; this great vault somehow speaks powerfully to the polygonal ends of the transepts. The choir vaulting is similar. At the eastern end is the ambulatory and elements of the

Early English work can just be seen here. The south-eastern chapel is entered via the south choir aisle and is dedicated to Blessed John Schorne. Schorne was Rector of North Marston in Buckinghamshire and it is said that he conjured the devil into a boot. He died in 1314 but his remains and his healing cult were moved here in 1478–80.

The furnishings of the chapel are extraordinarily rich. The reredos is by Sir Gilbert Scott and the altarpiece of *The Last Supper* by Benjamin West. The present east window's stained glass is by Clayton and Bell in memory of Prince Albert. The stalls are of 1478–84 and carved by William Berkeley. In four clearly stratified tiers – they are, coming from the back, the Garter Knights, the Military Knights, the minor canons and choirmen, and finally the choirboys in the very front row. Above the back row are elaborate canopies with helmets and crests mounted upon them. The Garter stall plates are themselves a heraldic treasure house – the best are a group of twenty-seven dating from 1415 and cut in the shape of the heraldic design. The sculptuary is remarkable and a study in itself. The eastern ambulatory doors to the former Henry III chapel are particularly fine elegant scrollwork, dating from 1248.

The chantry chapel of the First Lord Hastings (the oldest barony in England) has lierne vaulting dating from 1503, although Hastings had been beheaded by Richard III in 1483. The King George VI memorial chapel, in a form of modernised Perpendicular, by George Pace with Paul Paget of Seely and Paget, is remarkably successful especially remembering the sensitivity of the commission. There is also within the chapel a monument to Princess Margaret in Caithness stone by Richard Kindersley. The nave canons' stalls and screen are also by George Pace (1971–2) and the semicircular Knights and Choir Stalls are by Robert Maguire (1978). The great west window is very fine with seventy-five figures, all of which bar seven are original work of 1500–15 by Netherlands artists, but under the aegis of the King's Glazier, Barnard Flower.

The environs of the chapel are also of considerable interest. To the north-west is the Horseshoe Cloister, not really a cloister at all but built in 1478–81 as houses for Priest Vicars. There is a variety of other houses including the Marbeck, an irregular red brick canon's house of the early eighteenth century. The Vicars' Hall is to the north of the Horseshoe Cloister and was taken over as the Chapter Library from 1705–1999. On the upper floor it includes a large room with an open tie beam roof. To the east is St George's House rebuilt as a small college in the 1960s. Further east still are the Dean's and Canons' Cloisters, both of the thirteenth and fourteenth centuries. Henry III's chapel was replaced in 1494–8 by what is now called the Albert Memorial Chapel.

Below: The interior with fan vaulting.

AYLESFORD PRIORY

The Carmelite friars first came to Aylesford in 1242, and alongside Hulne at Alnwick, it was one of the first priories established by the order in England. It was Richard de Grey who gave land for a priory. The first church was dedicated in 1248. In *c.*1280 the Pilgrims' Hall, a guest house, was built. At the beginning of the fourteenth century, following generous endowments, rebuilding began. The church was begun in 1348 and completed in 1417. After the Reformation the priory eventually fell into the hands of Sir John Sedley, who converted it into a country house. During the 1930s the then owner restored much of the complex to its medieval monastic style. The fifteenth-century gatehouse survives along with the four-bay south and west walks of the cloister. In the south-west corner is the wide arch of the former watergate.

Carmelite friars returned to Aylesford Priory in 1949. The restored refectory became the chapel and eventually the buildings were transformed. The Pilgrims' Hall has reverted to its original use and, in 1965, Adrian Gilbert Scott's new shrine for the remains of St Simon Stock and associated chapels were consecrated. Also within the grounds is a fine seventeenth-century thatched tithe barn which now acts as a tearoom and shop.

Above: Looking across the courtyard towards the Prior's Hall.

MICHELHAM PRIORY

Understanding the layout of the former priory here is more challenging, since so much is lost, but one's visit is more than compensated for by the beauty of the location and present buildings. Founded in 1229 for thirteen Augustinian canons, the arrangement was traditional with a gatehouse, substantial cruciform church (63 metres/206 feet), cloister with a dormitory range, refectory and prior's lodgings, all set within a moated enclosure. At the Dissolution, in 1537, the church and eastern range were immediately demolished. The prior's lodgings, however, were transformed into a private house for the Foote family who took it over from Thomas Cromwell. Numerous alterations followed in ensuing centuries, including the building of a south-west wing. The priory is now in the care of the Sussex Archaeological Society.

The approach is over a sixteenth-century bridge, through the broad fifteenth-century monastic gatehouse. One then directly faces the south part of the prior's lodgings, albeit significantly adapted. The west wall of the former refectory is visible from the main staircase, and doorways lead into the refectory, which borders the site of the former cloister now marked out by a rose garden. A late sixteenth-century barn lies to the south-west as well as the foundations of a *c.*1280–1350 hall to the east of the barn.

Above: The gatehouse.

BATTLE ABBEY

The significance for English history of the Battle of Hastings, of the year 1066, and of the subsequent Norman Conquest, can hardly be exaggerated. The cultural implications were enormous, not least in the development of ecclesiastical architecture. It appears that Battle Abbey was built on this site, on Senlac Hill, the site of the battle, as a penance imposed by the Papal authorities in 1070 for the bloodshed caused by the Norman invasion. Tradition has it that the high altar of the abbey church was placed at exactly the point where King Harold died in the battle.

There are virtually no signs of the abbey church now above ground, but parts of the former monastery were converted and modernised by Sir Anthony Browne, Henry VIII's Master of Horse, into a country residence in the 1530s. In the twentieth century, it was once again transformed into a girls' public school, which is effectively what we see now. The building of the abbey began *c.*1070 and was finished around two decades later. Battle was a Benedictine foundation and it was further extended and added to in the twelfth century, and again later. A refashioned east end with chevet chapels was built on to the church in the late thirteenth century, after the style of Westminster Abbey.

The most significant remains still visible are those of the great gatehouse, the western range (the part of the building that was converted), the eastern range with the reredorter and associated rooms, and finally the guest range. The gatehouse is one of the finest examples of a monastic gatehouse in England. In its present form, in the Decorated style, it dates from 1338 and many of the medieval chambers within it remain. The precinct walls stand east of the gatehouse range and were built by Abbot Ralph (1107–1124). This brings us to the site of the church, which was some 68 metres (223 feet) long, and had a west front with slender towers. As was the tradition at that time, the presbytery had an apsidal end with an ambulatory with radiating chapels. The lower courses of the chapter house survive, including the stone benches, as do parts of the impressive dormitory range with its undercroft.

The outline of the cloister is still visible, now marked with gravel paths. The most splendid survival in the eastern range is the loftily vaulted novices' chamber; signs of the Early English work are clear in the lancets at the southern end of this range. The western range of the abbey was rebuilt in the thirteenth century and it includes the Great Hall. The guest range was extensively rebuilt after the Reformation by Sir Anthony Browne, and the two western corner towers are all that remain from this period of rebuilding. The original abbot's great hall lay parallel to the cloister with the abbot's chamber at right angles to the west. South west of the gatehouse is the visitor centre of 2007.

Below: Viewed from the south-east.

ST AUGUSTINE'S ABBEY, CANTERBURY

n 597, Augustine arrived on the coast of Kent. A rather reluctant missionary by all accounts, he preferred the warmer climate and the more cultured inhabitants at Autun in Burgundy, where he had tarried awhile on his way from Rome. He had been despatched to the country of the Angles and Saxons by Pope Gregory the Great, whose instructions to Augustine are recorded by the Venerable Bede in his *Ecclesiastical History of England*. His first key task was to convert Ethelbert, King of Kent, to Christianity. This he achieved with the support of Ethelbert's wife, Bertha, who was already a Christian believer.

As well as establishing his cathedral in Canterbury (almost certainly under the north nave aisle of the present building), he founded a Benedictine abbey as a base for his monks, outside the walls of the city and to the east. Legend has it that King Ethelbert gave the land which had been the site of the king's own Pagan temple for the monastery. The original buildings will have been of timber after the pattern of Anglo-Saxon monasteries; later, a stone building replaced the wooden structures. The first church was consecrated in 613. In 624, Eadbald, Ethelbert's son and successor constructed a second church just to the east and dedicated it to the Blessed Virgin Mary. The abbey became known as St Augustine's after the founder's death. For two centuries, the abbey remained the only significant religious house in the kingdom of Kent. It was Dunstan who, in the mid tenth century, reorganised the abbey under the Benedictine rule.

Some of the seventh- to eight-century walling of the abbey survives on the abbey site. It was the first Norman abbot, Scolland, who would take forward the building of a new abbey, razing the Saxon buildings to the ground. A new presbytery with crypt, on the site of the former St Mary's church, had been completed by the time of Scolland's death in 1087. The crypt survives within the abbey site. The nave, with its twin western towers was finished in *c.*1120.

The monastic precinct was to the north of the church and included a great cloister 37 metres (120 feet) square, alongside which was a rectangular chapter house of the twelfth century, but rebuilt in 1324–32.

The site of the dormitory can just be seen, but of the refectory hardly anything survives. The Fyndon Gate, the great gate to the monastery was constructed *c.*1300–08.

The visitor is aided enormously by the splendid Interpretation Building, by Heyningen and Haward and opened in 1997, just in time for the 1400th anniversary of Augustine's arrival.

Above: Looking towards the nave wall and arcading.

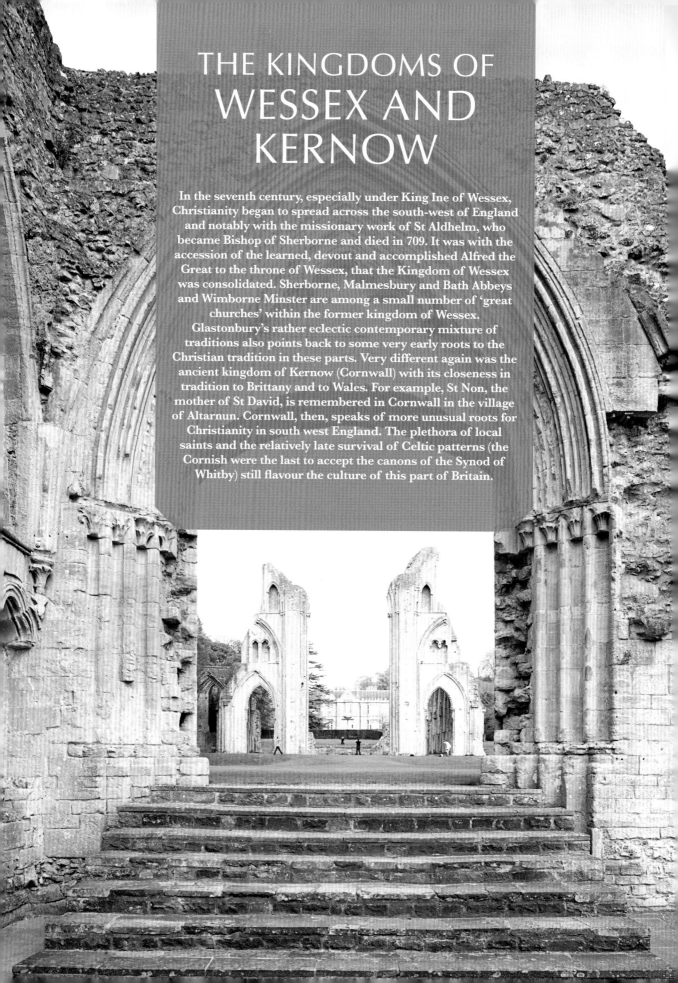

THE KINGDOMS OF WESSEX AND KERNOW

In the seventh century, especially under King Ine of Wessex, Christianity began to spread across the south-west of England and notably with the missionary work of St Aldhelm, who became Bishop of Sherborne and died in 709. It was with the accession of the learned, devout and accomplished Alfred the Great to the throne of Wessex, that the Kingdom of Wessex was consolidated. Sherborne, Malmesbury and Bath Abbeys and Wimborne Minster are among a small number of 'great churches' within the former kingdom of Wessex. Glastonbury's rather eclectic contemporary mixture of traditions also points back to some very early roots to the Christian tradition in these parts. Very different again was the ancient kingdom of Kernow (Cornwall) with its closeness in tradition to Brittany and to Wales. For example, St Non, the mother of St David, is remembered in Cornwall in the village of Altarnun. Cornwall, then, speaks of more unusual roots for Christianity in south west England. The plethora of local saints and the relatively late survival of Celtic patterns (the Cornish were the last to accept the canons of the Synod of Whitby) still flavour the culture of this part of Britain.

ROMSEY ABBEY

The Christian roots of Romsey Abbey run deep, probably embracing a Saxon double monastery of the ninth century. Certainly there is evidence that King Edmund the Elder established a convent for women in *c.*907. The present abbey was begun in 1120 as the focus of a Benedictine women's community. The twelfth-century Romanesque work has survived at all three levels – ground, triforium and clerestory. It is a clean rendition of this style with a feeling of spaciousness. Around 1300, the east end was remodelled, with two large Decorated Gothic windows surmounting the two Romanesque arches behind the high altar. There is a fine Romanesque triforium and clerestory windows above, and the tower, too, has some good detailed arcading. The nave reflects similar patterns to the east end, making the building of a piece. The manner in which the arches run into the giant piers is understandably complex and is similar to that in Jedburgh Abbey (see page 73) – interestingly the aunt of Kind David I of Scotland was a nun at Romsey. The transepts also follow a similar pattern. The north transept roof is by Benjamin Ferrey and was completed in 1865.

At the Dissolution of the Monasteries the church was bought by the town, which saved it from demolition. The wooden barrel vault in the nave is of 1860. Outside on the west wall of the south transept is the celebrated Romsey rood, pre-Romanesque in its origins.

The successive owners of nearby Broadlands have brought glory to the abbey and town, including the fine St Barbe tomb of 1658, the statue of Lord Palmerston in the Market Place, and the tomb recalling Lord Mountbatten's tragic assassination in 1979.

Below: The south-west facade of Romsey Abbey.
Opposite: Glastonbury Abbey.

MALMESBURY ABBEY

almesbury is one of very few English monasteries with a continuous history reaching back to the seventh century. The site was chosen by an Irish monk, Maildubh, who set up a hermitage but also taught local children. It was then refounded, as a Benedictine monastery, *c.*676 by Aldhelm, a seventh-century monk, and later Bishop of Wessex and later still canonised. Aldhelm also founded Sherborne Abbey. Rather quirkily, Malmesbury Abbey was the site of an early attempt at human flight, when Eilmer, a monk of the abbey flew from the tower for some 200 metres (650 feet) before landing, when he broke both legs. Later, he commented that the reason for the brevity of his flight was the lack of a tailplane on his glider!

The splendid space of the nave, which dates from 1160, with its pointed Transitional arcades and rounded Norman triforium, along with the porch, are but fragments of what was originally a vast cruciform church. Until 1500, a spire, some 131 metres (430 feet) high, taller than that at Salisbury Cathedral, crowned the crossing tower; with the tower beneath it, this collapsed *c.*1500 destroying much of the church. There was also a very large western tower which collapsed around the time of the Dissolution. The east wall of the church stands where the screen at the crossing once stood. Outside, the arch into the north transept still survives. Also externally, the

Romanesque blind arcading on the west front still points to the majesty of the building. The Norman carvings above the south porch are the glory of Malmesbury. Indeed, the sculptures here appear as one of the best collections of Romanesque art in England even though some of the outer porch is badly weathered. It is thought that the figures are the work of an internationally experienced and widely cultured sculptor. The six apostles on each side have influenced twentieth-century English sculpture and painting.

One of the curious features of the abbey is the box-like structure at triforium level on the south side of the nave; it is not certain whether it was there as an observation post or as a place of penance. Malmesbury has associations with two significant figures from the past – the tomb commemorating King Athelstan (king of England from 925–39) is at the eastern end of the north aisle, and William of Malmesbury, arguably the greatest English historian between Bede and Gibbon, spent nearly his whole life in the monastery. The abbey had gained a celebrated reputation as a centre for academic learning under the rule of abbots including Aldhelm himself, John Scotus Eriugena (a well-known early schoolman), Alfred of Malmesbury and Aelfric of Eynsham.

The Romanesque nave survives as the parish church.

Below: The nave, now serving as a parish church.

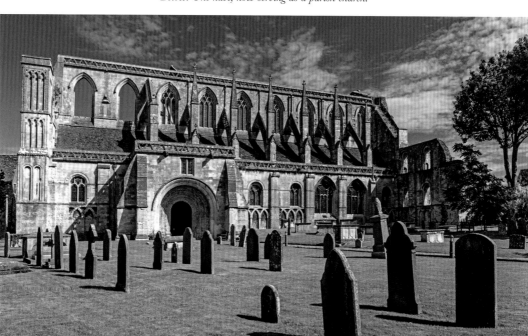

BATH ABBEY

Bath's Christian roots go back to the Roman origins of the town, but the first certain recorded date is of 757, where the monastery of St Peter in Bath is mentioned; in time a Benedictine community was established. It was here, in 973, that Edgar was crowned the first king of all England, commemorated by Queen Elizabeth II's visit in 1973. In 1090, Bishop John de Villula of Wells moved his seat to Bath and began building a great Romanesque cathedral and abbey buildings. The cathedral, half as long again as the present abbey, was completed around 1170, and some fragments of the stone of this abbey church can be seen in Bath Abbey Heritage Vaults Museum. The only real sign of this earlier building visible in the present abbey is a round-headed arch in the east wall of the so-called Norman Chapel. In 1244 the diocese

transferred back to Wells and Bath's influence waned, although the diocese is still called Bath and Wells with diocesan events focused on Bath.

It was in 1499, with the initiative of Bishop Oliver King, that Bath Abbey moved back into prominence. King began the present church, which was the last major Perpendicular building in England and the apotheosis of the Perpendicular style. This can be appreciated in the nobility of the west front with its fine carvings, including Oliver King's rebus of the olive tree and the crown, and his splendid vision of ascending angels. Inside the building, apart from the sense of height, the great triumph is the glorious fan vaulting of local Bath stone. This effusion of Perpendicular extravagance is continued in the

Above: Viewed from the south.

Above: The choir.

chantry chapel of Prior William Bird, who died in 1525. The slender Jesse window in the south transept extends from the tomb of Sir William Waller to the vaulting above. The choir now boasts fine new acoustic screens (2005). Gilbert Scott did remarkable work on the building, starting in 1850 and this included the glorious vaulting which he restored to the nave.

Bath is justly famous for its memorials and plaques. In the south nave aisle is the burial place of Beau Nash, who helped establish the reputation of the city as a spa in the eighteenth century. In 1997, the Chapel of St Alphege was consecrated, commemorating Bath's most celebrated abbot, who became Archbishop of Canterbury and was martyred in the early part of the eleventh century. The statue by Lawrence Tindall, of Christ's resurrection (2000), is close to the south-east door.

Bath Abbey has seen some of the most imaginative conservation and innovation work on any English abbey church in recent years. The nineteenth-century pews in the nave, placed there at the time of Gilbert Scott's remarkable restoration work, have been removed revealing the pier bases and ledger stones and the north floor of the nave has been saved. Bath's hot springs are now used to heat the abbey and the underground vaults to the south of the abbey now provide new facilities.

SHERBORNE ABBEY

The former episcopal see of Wessex was established under the Saxon King, Ine. Thus Sherborne Abbey's history begins with the establishment of that diocese with Aldhelm, Abbot of Malmesbury, as its first bishop in 705. The Saxon building became both a Benedictine abbey church and a cathedral in 998 with the introduction of a community of monks under the aegis of Bishop Wulfsin. The see lasted for almost 400 years. In 1058 Ramsbury was joined with Sherborne but in 1075, following the Norman Conquest, the diocese was given a new centre at Old Sarum.

The present Anglo-Saxon remains appear to date from *c.*1045 and Saxon stonework is still visible in the abbey. The core of the crossing, the Saxon west wall and the 'westwork', with the doorway at the west end of the north aisle is from this period. The Norman rebuilding probably began in the first half of the twelfth century and elements of this can be seen in the arches at the crossing and in the walls of the transepts, behind the later Perpendicular framework. Almost certainly the Normans added aisles to what had been an aisleless nave, and there is evidence that Norman choir aisles were added in the late twelfth century. Early in the thirteenth century, a Lady Chapel was added axially at the east end. This was replaced in the fifteenth century by the chapel of St Mary le Bow and finally, the present Gothic chapel designed by Caroe, was completed in 1921. In the fourteenth century a new church was built abutting the west end of the abbey church; this church of All Hallows was built for the townsfolk and demolished in 1540. This followed a long period of serious conflict between the town and the abbey causing much of the abbey to be burnt.

The abbey church was rebuilt in Perpendicular style in the mid fifteenth century, following the damage from the dispute with the town. The nave arcading is unusual and is probably a Perpendicular rebuilding of the earlier Norman work; this would account for the great thickness of the pillars, caused by panelling being added to a Romanesque core. The nave and choir fan vaulting are the triumph of the building and in the nave the vault is supported by neither pinnacles nor flying buttresses. There is an intricate pattern of ribs with carved bosses where they cross. The design of the vaulting in the choir is even more daring, with transverse ribs that are almost flat; in the mid nineteenth century flying buttresses were added to protect the roof from collapse. The west front includes Saxon, Norman and Perpendicular work, as does the central tower. The west window by John Hayward, with the Madonna as its central focus, is a triumph. Hayward produced a second window for the south nave aisle and, in 2005, a statue of St Aldhelm was completed by Marzia Colonna for the vacant niche in the front porch.

Below: Viewed from the south-west.

MILTON ABBEY

The earliest abbey was founded *c*.933 by King Athelstan for secular clerks, but only thirty-one years later it was refounded as a Benedictine abbey. The Normans built a larger church but only fragments have survived from its destruction by fire in 1309. The church and the hall of Abbot Middleton (1481–1525) are all that remain of the former monastery. Construction of the new church began in 1310 but there were pauses partly caused by the Black Death. The tower was not completed until the mid fifteenth century. The retrochoir, ambulatory, Lady Chapel, and chapels flanking it, all disappeared at the Dissolution. Abbot Middleton's strenuous efforts to complete the church were successful as far as the crossing and transepts.

Despite evidence of some footings, it is clear that the nave was never started. The abbey church is unusual in the lateness of its building, close to the calamitous events of the sixteenth century.

Nonetheless, despite this, the architecture is fine – both of the exterior and interior. The great south window is particularly impressive, with its seven lights, and there is fan vaulting at the crossing. There are five fourteenth- to fifteenth-century misericords and a fourteenth-century pulpitum with a rib-vaulted passage. The monastic buildings were converted into the mansion of Sir John Tregonwell. The buildings are now, of course, used as a co-educational public school.

Below: The nave.

CHRISTCHURCH PRIORY

There had been a Saxon minster of some sort on this site from the ninth century, but the present priory dates from the time of Ranulph Flambard who began the rebuilding *c.*1090. It became an Augustinian foundation in 1150 and there was further building in the late twelfth and early thirteenth centuries. The Lady Chapel is fourteenth-century and the choir early sixteenth. The north transept is Christchurch's crowning glory with extraordinary ornamentation.

We can trace the size of the extensive monastic house from the proportions of the church, which is some 95 metres (311 feet) long. The vaulted nave is of seven bays with Romanesque arcading probably from the 1130s. The Norman clerestory was replaced by 'two light' Early English windows; the vaulting is plaster by William Garbett 1819. The aisles were remodelled in the thirteenth century with rib vaulting. The choir is four bays long and the

Lady Chapel three bays with similar vaulting to the choir. The north porch is monumental in scale and vaulted in two bays with an interesting tympanum above the twin portals. The fifteenth-century west tower is fine and restrained – it is approximately 40 metres (130 feet) in height. There are three crypts, which are the oldest parts of the fabric, one extending beneath the choir.

Above: The nave and west tower.

CLEEVE ABBEY

Set within a beautiful valley near Washford in Somerset, Cleeve is unusual since the church has gone but substantial remains of the monastic buildings survive. The abbey was founded by William de Roumere, Earl of Lincoln, for the Cistercians, originally as a daughter house of Revesby in Lincolnshire. Set by the river in a typically Cistercian location, the thirteenth-century monastic buildings offer a unique glimpse of the life of a medieval Cistercian house. The line of the cloister roofs can be seen on three sides, the eastern range containing the chapter house, the library and the sacristy. Close to these is the day stair to the dormitory, which is preserved exceptionally complete. It stretches the entire length of the upper floor.

The south range included the demolished old refectory. The new refectory is undoubtedly the glory of the abbey and perhaps the most splendid room in Somerset. It dates to the 1460s and includes the angel roof with angels holding shields supporting the roof trusses. The stone corbels are also carved with angels and there is a carved vine trail on the wall plates. The large east wall painting of the Crucifixion has disappeared. The thirteenth-century gatehouse at the north-west corner of the precinct was rebuilt by Abbot Dovell in the early sixteenth century.

Above: The gatehouse.

WIMBORNE MINSTER

The origin of Wimborne Minster lies in a Saxon monastery founded by Cuthburga in 705. Cuthburga was the sister of King Ine of Wessex who was also responsible for founding Sherborne Abbey. Later a Benedictine abbey church probably occupied the same site as the present minster. King Alfred the Great buried his brother, King Aethered, in the minster in 871 and the Saxon church survived until it was burnt by the Danes in 1013. St Walpurga was educated in the monastery where she lived for twenty-six years before becoming a missionary in Germany at the behest of her mother's brother, St Boniface – Boniface was later martyred and his shrine is in Fulda in Hesse. In 1043 Edward the Confessor established a new foundation of secular canons on the site. The minster was declared a deanery by Henry III and then a free chapel by Edward II, thus exempting it from normal ecclesiastical jurisdiction. None of the collegiate buildings remain, except for the church, which has survived complete.

On the outside, the church is dominated by the western and central towers. The central crossing tower dates from the late twelfth century but its foundations probably date back to the earlier Saxon church and was originally faced with limestone, but continued repairs have left it with rather varied colouring. Romanesque work is clearly visible on the exterior of the tower. The Perpendicular western tower is *c.*1464, and houses a peal of ten bells.

Entering the church through the north porch, it is best first to visit the baptistry, beneath the western tower. Here there is a fascinating fourteenth-century astronomical clock. The arches from the baptistry into the nave are Decorated in style and date from around 1350. The nave is Norman but with the first three arcades in the late pointed Transitional style, while the final arcades on the north and south sides nearer the crossings are Romanesque.

The crossing instils an air of Norman nobility, with the arches in plain Romanesque style, although it may go back to the Saxon-Norman foundations of its predecessor. The basis of both transepts is also Norman, but each has been extended. The north transept was refashioned in 1350 by Dean Brembre in the Decorated style, and the south in 1220 along with the chancel. The great east window with its three lancets is a beautiful example of Early English work. Wyatt is responsible for the Perpendicular clerestory in the mid nineteenth century.

Wimborne contains two other gems, one of which is the splendid crypt which forms the Lady Chapel and dates from 1340. The Bankes family of Corfe Castle and Kingston Lacy have their burial vaults here. The other gem is on the south side above the choir vestry; here is a small chained library of 240 books, almost a miniature version of the one at Hereford. Also interesting are the tombs of Daniel Defoe's two daughters, in St George's Chapel on the north side of the chancel.

Below: Viewed from the south-west.

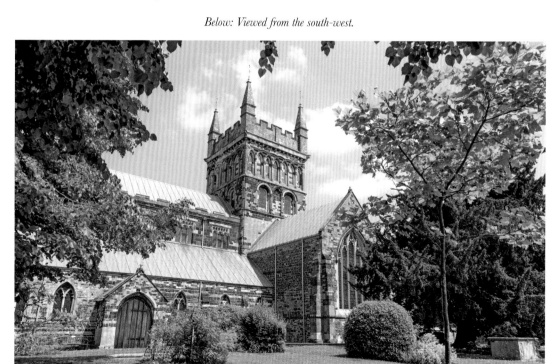

BEAULIEU ABBEY

lthough originally the largest Cistercian house in England, sadly very little of the church survives, but there are still in existence some elements of the former monastery, including the former refectory, now serving as the parish church. At its height, the abbey held much prestige with four daughter houses being spawned by it: nearby Netley, Newenham in Devon, St Mary Graces in London and Hailes in Gloucestershire (see page 38); Hailes later became one of the most significant focuses for pilgrimage in mediaeval England. This was almost entirely due to the phial of the Holy Blood brought there by Edmund, son of Richard of Cornwall.

Beaulieu Abbey was founded by King John in 1204 with a cluster of monks coming from Cîteaux in south-west France, the mother house of the Cistercian order. The church was completed in 1227 and finally consecrated in 1246 in the presence of Henry III. It was vast, some 102 metres (330 feet) in length, and its ground plan is marked out in situ. Built of Binstead stone from near Quarr Abbey on the Isle of Wight, it was of the later Cistercian plan with an eastern end which included an ambulatory and radiating chapels. All that remains of this glorious church is the lower section of the south aisle wall.

The cloister east range includes the Chapter House entrance, which was extensively conserved in 2015–16. On the eastern side of the cloister, there is an oval stone memorial in one of the recesses for members of the Special Operations Executive who

trained at Beaulieu in the Second World War. The former refectory is now used as the parish church, and the fine pulpit in the west wall, from which a book would have been read during meals, is an attractive surviving feature. The building dates from 1230 and remains much as it would have appeared, but for the addition of a small bell-turret of c.1730.

Some of the original lancet windows survive in the cloister's west range – this would have been the lay brothers' quarters with a dormitory above and a refectory below. Between this cloister west walk and the lay brothers' range ran a lane, which was effectively their cloister – the doorway here was their access to the church. The thirteenth-century monastic gatehouse (refashioned in the mid fourteenth century) was converted into a hunting lodge after the Dissolution (now known as Palace House) by Thomas Wriothesley, later, Earl of Southampton. Elements of the former gatehouse remain in the converted building. The estate later passed into the hands of the Montagu family who remain the owners; the third Lord Montagu of Beaulieu founded the National Motor Museum in 1952.

With the abbey ruins, the parish church, the National Motor Museum and Buckler's Hard close by, there is much of interest in and around the village. Buckler's Hard was one of the most significant shipbuilding centres in England, reaching the climax of its fame in the late eighteenth century.

Above: The cloister and receptors (now a parish church).

Above: The crossing pillar.

GLASTONBURY ABBEY

Surrounding Glastonbury are many well-known legends of Celtic saints, of King Arthur, and of Joseph of Arimathea introduced from the late twelfth century to encourage donations and pilgrimage, and to enhance the status of the English Church in Western Europe. However, there was a religious settlement here before a Saxon king added a stone church around 700. Indeed, there is pottery evidence for occupation of this site going back as far as the third or fourth centuries and so within Roman times. The first church was on the site of the present Lady Chapel and was a timber building. There was a holy well outside the south wall of the church. King Ine of the West Saxons built a second church in 712–719, dedicated to St Peter and St Paul, just to the east of the original building. The earliest archaeological evidence for the making of glass in England *c.*680 has been confirmed by radio carbon dating of material discovered in the 1950s.

Abbot Dunstan enlarged the church and added an eastern tower in the mid tenth century. Oddly, after the Norman Conquest, the original church was retained, but the church of Ine and Dunstan disappeared beneath the nave of a still larger church of Romanesque style built by Abbot Herlewin *c.*1110. This church was completed in the mid twelfth century, by Henry of Blois, along with a cloister and other conventual buildings. The whole of this complex was burnt down in a serious fire in 1184,

but miraculously the rebuilding was complete to allow for the Lady Chapel to be consecrated in 1186.

The completed abbey was not consecrated until the end of the medieval period. The programme of rebuilding was long and complex: the crossing tower was finished in the early fourteenth century and the cloisters were rebuilt at the beginning of the fifteenth century. A crypt was built beneath the Lady Chapel with access to the holy well just outside the building. This was to accommodate the cult of Joseph of Arimathea. The church was of enormous proportions with a nave of 177 metres (580 feet) – 10 metres longer than the nave of Canterbury Cathedral. The completed building was a mixture of Romanesque and Gothic. This new church, beginning at its west end in the fully developed Romanesque style, was not consecrated until the mid fourteenth century. Of the Romanesque work remaining, the Lady Chapel, especially its north door, is very fine. The abbey gatehouse survives leading into the Market Square. Two of the crossing piers still dominate this evocative ruin; the kitchen of the abbot's house (mid fourteenth-century) has a vaulted lantern roof.

Irish scholars taught St Dunstan here in the early tenth century and as abbot of a new community, he reintroduced the Rule of St Benedict. In recent times, alongside the contemporary music festival, a great variety of religious and mystical traditions are represented in the town.

Below: Glastonbuy Abbey park and ruins.

BUCKFAST ABBEY

The history of Buckfast Abbey is remarkable, with the most recent phase of its existence, (this time as a Benedictine house) beginning in 1882, when monks from the French monastery of St Pierre-qui-Vire, re-established the foundation with further support from German novices. An abbey existed here, however, as far back as Saxon times. Later a monastery was founded in 1018, so before the Norman Conquest. As part of a monastic reform movement in the twelfth century, Buckfast became a Sauvignac Cistercian monastery, in 1134. This foundation was then suppressed during the Dissolution in 1539.

The buildings gradually fell into a state of disrepair until the nineteenth century, when Samuel Berry built a romantic Gothic castle-like mansion where the eastern range had stood. When Buckfast was resettled by Benedictine monks from France, initially they took over this curious mansion. Fairly quickly, they excavated the medieval site as they began to follow precisely the original plan in the rebuilding of the monastery. It is the present chapter house, first constructed as the temporary church that heralds the visitor today.

It was the initiative of Abbot Anscar Vonier, the second abbot of the restored monastery, which led to the remarkable rebuilding of the abbey by the monks themselves. Building began in 1907 and was completed in 1937, with the layout conforming exactly to the ground plan of the original monastery. The main walls are of local blue limestone and the window arches, quoins, coping stones and tower turrets are of mellow Ham Hill stone from Somerset. The architectural style is a mixture of Romanesque and early Gothic.

The Abbot's tower (c.fourteenth century) is connected to the Berry Mansion and has a double-centred archway – F.A. Walters was the main architect for the new work. The church is large, 70 metres (230 feet) long, with aisles and one chapel in each transept. Generally, the style is a mixture of English Cistercian and early French Gothic – the proportions of the tower are Perpendicular.

Remains of the medieval monastery include the Northgate and the undercroft chapel of St Michael (both twelfth-century) and, from the fourteenth and fifteenth centuries, the guest hall and south gate.

There is a shop north of the guest hall by Richard Riley 1983. It takes the form of a large barn-like gatehouse. The abbey is the third most popular tourist destination in south-west England, with as many as 400,000 visitors each year. The restaurant, also by Riley, was opened in 1991.

Below: A view of the rebuilt abbey from the north-west.

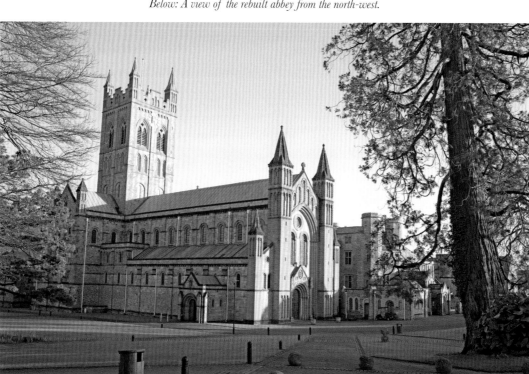

ST GERMAN'S PRIORY

For a variety of different reasons, in Cornwall, there are very few priories or abbeys with evidence surviving above the ground. The priory church of St Germans and the conventual buildings absorbed into Port Eliot House are thus of particular importance. More of the church here survives than of other monastic churches in the county. Tradition has it that St Germanus of Auxerre founded the earliest monastery c.430. Certainly, St Germans was the cathedral church of Anglo-Saxon Cornwall, and bishops are known from 930–1040. Thereafter it merged with Crediton and the see moved to Exeter. In 1161, it became an Augustinian priory and this building was consecrated in 1261.

The west front is flanked by two towers. The north tower becomes octagonal in its second storey and is lower than the southern one. The great glory of the building is the western portal with its seven orders including impressive chevron carving. The south elevation of the church contrasts with the otherwise plainness of the west front. It is battlemented and buttressed with five large windows. Much of the interior is from the later Middle Ages. Next door, Port Eliot house used the north range of the claustral buildings and three lancets remain from the former undercroft. At its east end the house was attached to the prior's lodgings.

Above: The west front.

[71]

SCOTLAND

Some of the essential roots of both Scottish and English history are traced well north of the border with the advent of Columba and Aidan. Equally, a number of the Scottish abbeys and notably within the Cistercian tradition, were founded as daughter houses of English monasteries. Even so, the Scottish Reformation took a very different path to that in England.

Sadly, the impact on the monastic inheritance was equally catastrophic. Still, remarkable ruins survive. Three out of four of the 'Border Abbeys', as those on the eastern border are known, are still panoramic in their ruinous state. Each one is of a different observance, but Dryburgh, Melrose and Jedburgh are all arresting in their own way; even Kelso remains majestic through its surviving tower. In Galloway, the abbeys of Dundrennan and Sweetheart are impressive and Holyrood, flanking the great palace, reminds one of the link between royalty and religion. Indeed, it was the devotion of Queen Margaret that energised David I, her son, into establishing so many of the great twelfth-century foundations. Iona stands alone in more than one sense, because of its island location, but its place in Scotland's Christian history offers an incomparable uniqueness. Like Pluscarden, it also is still a living foundation.

JEDBURGH ABBEY

The Roman road known as Dere Street, running through Rochester in Northumberland and past Catcleugh reservoir, brings one into the ancient town of Jedburgh which was an Anglo-Saxon town and within the ancient kingdom of Northumbria. Travelling into Jedburgh on Dere Street, the abbey, by virtue of its height, position and surviving buildings, is without a doubt the most impressive of the four border abbeys. Set on several terraces above the Jed Water, it confronts the traveller, as doubtless King David I of Scotland intended, when he established the Augustinian monastery *c.*1138.

Tradition has it that the site has a long monastic history reaching back to the early ninth century when Bishop Ecgred gave the grant to the monastery at Lindisfarne to build here; archaeological finds support this tradition.

The first monks for the Augustinian foundation came from St Quentin at Beauvais in the Île-de-France. It became a full abbey *c.*1154. In the later part of the twelfth century there was an enormous programme of building when the presbytery was completely reconstructed; the nave was begun *c.*1180 and finished in the early thirteenth century. For obvious reasons, remembering the town's proximity to the border, the abbey was very vulnerable to attacks in the wars with England. In the sixteenth century the abbey came into the effective possession of the Home family, and the damaged monastic church was used as a parish church for a time after the Reformation. There has been much careful excavation of the site, most recently from 1983–86 and 1990, which have helped in finally clarifying the plan. The site is very well laid out by Historic Scotland.

There is sufficient of the abbey remaining to gain a very clear picture of the complete plan. The nave is impressive and remarkably homogeneous. The arcading is Gothic in style with a very tall gallery and the piers are formed of a series of eight grouped circular columns. One can gain a good vista of the nave by climbing the stairs which are set within the west front and take one to triforium level. That pattern of arcading changes significantly at the clerestory level. The west front survives to full height and there is an impressive doorway of six orders in Transitional style. The presbytery was entirely rebuilt in the 1170s, probably for structural reasons. The south choir aisle was reconstructed once again in the fifteenth century – Abbot John Hall's name is inscribed. The transepts also survive to a greater degree than in many ruined medieval monasteries. The tower, also surviving to a remarkable degree crowns the building with some majesty.

Less survives of the conventual buildings with little of the cloister to be seen. Nonetheless, once again the basic shape of the chapter house and conventual range can be seen, along with the refectory undercroft. The visitor centre has an excellent exhibition with an interesting collection of artefacts.

Opposite: Melrose Abbey.
Below: The nave and tower viewed from the south.

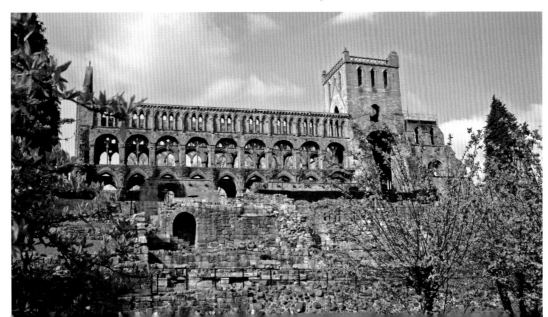

KELSO ABBEY

south arcade of the nave are visible, carried on squat cylindrical piers. Most important are the doorway through the west front and the north door through the wall of the north transept. The south and west faces of the western tower are the commanding features of the ruins of the abbey.

Of the monastic buildings nothing survives, save the outer parlour, next to the south transept. This is a rectangular chamber with a barrel vault. In 1975–76, to the south-east of the cloister, an excavation uncovered the site of the former monastic infirmary. Part of the abbey mill has been located 250 metres (820 feet) north-west of the abbey at the mouth of the lade, which brought water from the Tweed to the abbey. The Roxburghe Memorial cloister by Reginald Fairlie was constructed in 1933–4 with memorials to members of the Ducal family.

S adly, of all the four eastern Border abbeys, only a fragment of Kelso survives, although its majesty remains, at the end of Rennies's fine bridge over the Tweed. Founded by King David I, in 1113, it was for Tironesian monks. Here was probably the first of all Benedictine houses in Britain. The main survival as we now see it is of the western tower and its crossing. Two bays of the

Above: The memorial cloister.

COLDINGHAM PRIORY

C oldingham reaches back into those centuries when this part of Britain was re-evangelised by the northern saints. The present church and remains are on the site of the Anglo-Saxon double monastery established by St Aebbe sometime before 661–4. Indeed, it was also to here, in *c.*672, that Etheldreda, the Abbess of Ely came for some years. The Benedictine priory originated from a grant from King Edgar to Durham cathedral priory in *c.*1098. The church was dedicated in 1100 but then replaced in the late twelfth century by the present building. It was completed in the early thirteenth century, possibly delayed by an attack by King John.

The priory suffered particularly badly in the wars with England. What survives is effectively the choir of the priory church which would have originally had transepts and a nave to the west.

The east and north walls of the church are fine with fenestration high up, along with a wall passage.

Some of the south transept has survived but this has also been substantially rebuilt. Very little remains of the conventual buildings. The undercroft of the refectory was excavated in 1890–1. To the south of the refectory site are the remains of the chapter house. Within the space of the cloister garth, the footings of the inner walls of the walks have been located.

Above: The gateway and parish church.

DRYBURGH ABBEY

Undoubtedly the most beautifully set of all the abbeys in the eastern Borders, Dryburgh is set idyllically on bends in the river Tweed surrounded by stunning upland scenery. The origins are said to go back to St Modan (about whom we know very little), in the seventh century. The present foundation, however, is generally dated as 1150 when Hugh de Morville, a friend of King David I and Constable of Scotland, gave grant of the land. In 1152, canons arrived from Alnwick Abbey to establish what was probably the first Premonstratensian abbey in Scotland. There may just be traces of an earlier structure where the eastern conventual range abuts the church. Construction of the permanent buildings began towards the end of the twelfth century.

The abbey had a rocky start with a high spending abbot in the mid thirteenth century when debts are mentioned. Following this, the wars with England brought worse problems. It was burnt twice, in 1322 by Edward II of England and then in 1385 by Richard II. A further devasting fire afflicted the abbey later on, in 1461. Two further English attacks in 1523 and 1545 brought more serious damage.

The abbey church has an aisleless presbytery of three bays and then an aisled choir of two bays. The transepts have eastern chapel aisles and there was a tower at the crossing. The nave was eventually of six bays with irregular arcading and there was a screen wall across the nave at the second set of piers. The north side of the choir and adjoining north transept is the best preserved part of the church. The north choir and chapel aisles have quadripartite vaulting with the central boss showing Christ in Majesty. There are three stages and the middle stage is unusual with comparators only in Westminster Abbey and Hereford Cathedral. Little survives of the nave to any height, and it is impossible to offer conjecture over the design. The south eastern processional doorway has dogtoothing and is round-arched.

Of the conventual buildings, there are significant remains, with the eastern range being the most complete. The chapter house is gabled with three lancets and the sacristy lit by two round-headed windows – the parlour originally had a round-headed doorway. Part of the dormitory window survives on this side. The east range has barrel vaulting for the sacristy and library, as do the parlour and chapter house. The warming room comes next. The dormitory was above. The south range is filled almost entirely by the refectory with the kitchens at its north-east corner. It would appear that the western range was initially left unbuilt, doubtless on account of the early financial difficulties. In the sixteenth century buildings were added here, with three barrel-vaulted chambers.

Across the bridge to the south-west of the refectory are the remains of the two-storey gatehouse along with part of the north wall.

Among many fascinating memorials, are the tombs of Sir Walter Scott and his wife, and of Field Marshal Earl Haig.

Below: Looking across the graves to Dryburgh Abbey.

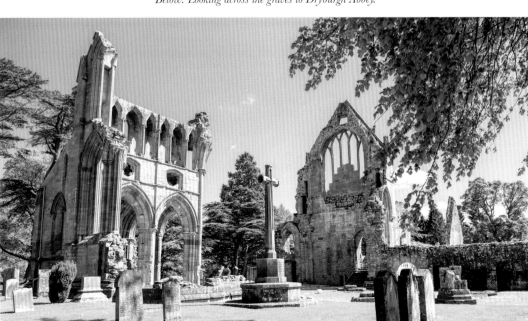

MELROSE ABBEY

The history of the abbey at Melrose takes us deep into the heart of the Northumbrian missions of the seventh century. It was from St Aidan's monastery at Old Melrose, when St Boisil (modern day St Boswell) was abbot, that St Cuthbert left for Lindisfarne as a missionary and later missionary bishop, in the kingdom of Northumbria. Old Melrose is just three miles to the east of modern Melrose within a bend in the River Tweed and below the bluff known as Scott's View. The ruins of the later abbey bring with them powerful resonances and still more so, as it is believed that the heart of King Robert Bruce is buried within the monastic grounds. A lead cask was found in 1921 and again in 1998, which is reputed to contain his heart, but is more likely to be the heart of a former abbot.

Old Melrose was a precursor of the Benedictine way, whereas Melrose, as we now see it, was the first Cistercian abbey in Scotland and of supreme importance in the development of Scottish monasticism. King David I, who was such a key influence in the building up of the monastic tradition north of the border was the founder. All but three of the other ten Cistercian foundations in Scotland stemmed from here. Melrose became Scotland's greatest producer and exporter of wool and is a good example of how Cistercianism was a powerhouse for industry. The first monks were from Rievaulx in north Yorkshire. They arrived here in 1136.

The beginning of construction began with the conventual buildings and just a temporary oratory. Nonetheless, by 1146, the eastern end of the abbey church was complete and was dedicated in that year. In the following half century other buildings were completed. The greatest setback came in 1385 with the assault of the abbey by English troops. This would occasion the entire rebuilding of the abbey, which would continue in two main phases throughout the fourteenth and fifteenth centuries. The new church was on a magnificent and splendid scale, much of which can be discerned from the very impressive ruins. This time, Richard II of England contributed to the works through a reduction in customs duty. The second phase sees the Scottish architectural heritage further influenced by mainland continental styles.

The 1136 church followed the Bernardine pattern from Clairvaux, but it is the later church which we see now, apart from the lower part of the west wall. The east end had by then moved on from the tradition of an apsidal pattern, with a chevet of chapels and an ambulatory, and so we see the later standard squared off east end. The nave is of seven bays but with a screen after the first four bays – the monastic choir was beyond the screen. The north nave aisle was very narrow. There was a galilee over the west entrance. The pier bases and capitals in the arcading are of three different patterns. There is a certain amount of surviving vaulting. The second and more 'continental' phase of building is picked up in the tracery of the east window and also in the doorways. The third phase (*c.*1430–1470) included the completion of the north transept. Just two further bays of the chapel aisle were completed after 1470. The west side of the crossing tower is all that survives.

Significant fragments of the conventual buildings remain although of the cloister walks themselves little can be ventured. The lower walls of the eastern claustral range give clarity to the plan, including the sequence of sacristy, chapter house, day stair, parlour,

Left: Arcading at Melrose Abbey.

Above: The nave and crossing from the south.

and what was probably the novices' day room. The latrine ran at right angles east of the range and would have been approached through the dormitory. The great monastic drain is perfectly preserved. Only fragments of the northern range are visible, and they were almost entirely occupied by the refectory on the first floor with a vaulted undercroft beneath. The lay brothers' accommodation was to the west of the cloister.

Foundations of what was almost certainly the abbot's hall have been excavated to the north-east of the cloister. To the west of this lay what was probably the commendator's house, dating from the mid fifteenth century (now the museum) and, just to the east of the cloister, within what later became a brewery complex, was the monk's infirmary.

In 1560, the Scottish Reformation meant the end of monastic life in the abbey and the estates came under the temporary 'Lordship' of John Ramsay,

Viscount Haddington. Parochial worship continued possibly in part of the abbey church. In *c.*1621, Thomas Hamilton, the Earl of Melrose caused a new church to be formed within the monastic choir and huge masonry piers were inserted on the north side. Eventually, in 1808, a new church was built elsewhere and the inserted walls were removed just leaving the barrel vault and north piers.

Since the eighteenth century, the abbey has been the focus of much artistic and historical inspiration, encouraged by the literary output of Sir Walter Scott. There is a celebrated watercolour of the abbey by J.M.W. Turner.

DUNDRENNAN ABBEY

L ess of the church survives here than of its daughter house of Sweetheart, also in Galloway. The best sources suggest that this was another foundation endowed by that great supporter of the burgeoning monastic life in the twelfth century, King David I. Cistercian records place its establishment as after that of Revesby in Lincolnshire which was founded in 1143. It may be that Dundrennan was the abbey founded by St Malachy in 1148, with the founding monks coming from Rievaulx, of which this was a daughter house. The first phase of building seems to have been completed *c.*1165 and the claustral buildings followed. The construction of the entire corpus was probably finished *c.*1200. Alan, Lord of Galloway, was buried at Dundrennan in 1234.

The presbytery was unaisled, and of four bays. Of the transepts, remains of the southern one are fragmentary, but the north transept is far more complete. The walls of the eastern transept chapels have largely disappeared – there were three chapels in each transept. Of the nave, we see only the lower courses of the side walls and much of this is nineteenth-century 'restoration'. The lower western gable was also rebuilt in 1841–43 and the central great west door was unblocked and restored in the 1840s. The interior of the presbytery and transepts is fairly complete. It has an early Cistercian austerity about it but with the normal nobility and care for

which the order became known. Damaged elements of both the sedilia and piscina are visible. In the late twelfth century, the crossing and transepts were remodelled adding a new elegance. The triforium of the north transept is quite impressive, although it was never vaulted. The lower parts of the western crossing piers survive, again having been restored in the nineteenth century.

The nave and cloister buildings formed a square court, and on the eastern side, the chapter house wall survives in its first storey. Otherwise, the range is ruinous as indeed is the south. The western range originally housed the lay brothers although the range was rebuilt in the late fifteenth century. Conjecture suggests that by then the company of lay brothers had been disbanded. The range was restored and rebuilt in the 1840s. There are significant tombs and memorials. One thirteenth-century tomb is carved with a recumbent abbot depicted as having been stabbed in the chest. His feet rest upon a small figure of a man dressed only in kilt and shoes and with his intestines spilling out from a large wound in his side. Maybe this portrays the fate of the assassin who had murdered the abbot.

Mary, Queen of Scots spent her last night in Scotland here in 1568, following the disastrous Battle of Langside. She then crossed the Solway Firth to Workington before she was imprisoned by Elizabeth I of England.

Below: Dundrennan Abbey from the south.

DUNFERMLINE ABBEY

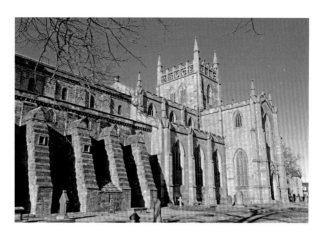

D unfermline Abbey points to two revolutions in Scottish religion and society. First came that of St Margaret, Queen of Scotland who, *c.*1070, brought Benedictine monks from Canterbury to found the priory here, which David I made an abbey in 1128. The second revolution was the Reformation, which is demonstrated starkly by the contrast between the homespun east end of the church, still a parish church, and the austere but impressive nave pointing to its former life. The church in an enlarged form was consecrated in 1150. The west front of the aisled nave is twelfth-century with the extraordinary unbalanced nature of the two western towers. The nave is of seven bays. The north door is twelfth-century with chevron decoration. The triforium, also twelfth-century, was round-arched. There is different coloured paving in the medieval nave. There is a painting of four apostles on the vault of the eastern bay of the north aisle, probably of the fifteenth century.

The cloister was to the south of the church and the south range was rebuilt in the early fourteenth century. Fragments of the south end of the east range survive, and of the reredorter and the refectory. The gatehouse lacks the poise and nobility of the refectory. The parish church is unashamedly a second church in Georgian perpendicular!

Above: The nave from the south.

PLUSCARDEN ABBEY

O ne of only three priories of the little known Valliscaulian order, Pluscarden lies in the valley of the Black Burn. Founded by King Alexander II *c.*1230, this observance stood between the Cistercian and Carthusian rules. The abbey had small a eastern limb forming the presbytery, then a crossing with a tower which was probably never completed. The transepts each had a two-bay eastern chapel aisle and a nave aisled only on the south side. The transepts show clear evidence of fire damage caused presumably by the conflagrations of either 1390 or 1402 due to attacks by either the Earl of Buchan or Alexander of the Isles. They have been walled off since 1961.

There is a claustral range, with sacristy, chapter house, parlour and refectory. In 1821, the then owner, the Earl of Fife, had the claustral range re-roofed. In 1898, the estates were bought by a Catholic convert, the Marquess of Bute; later, his son sold everything with the hope of re-establishing monastic life here. In 1945, the buildings were transferred to the Benedictine community at Prinknash and in 1974, they were given abbey status. Pluscarden offers two points of interest – the historic buildings and a living community of monks, whose new buildings add a further fascination.

Above: The rebuilt Pluscarden Abbey.

HOLYROOD ABBEY

One of the symbolic buildings of the 'Athens of the North' is Edinburgh's ancient Augustinian abbey. Once again, it was the energy and commitment of King David I which lay behind the abbey's foundation. It was his mother Queen Margaret – later St Margaret – who effectively gave the abbey its name. She venerated a relic which she believed to be part of the true cross, the Holy Rood. She had died in Edinburgh castle in 1093 and the Norman chapel from those times survives. David founded the abbey, dedicated to the Holy Rood, in 1128. This royal foundation gave Holyrood particular prestige. It remains a striking building and noble too – indeed later the cloister would form part of a Renaissance palace. The abbey was a daughter house of St Andrew's and one doorway into the cloister survives from this period.

The original design was surprisingly modest – an aisleless nave, short transept, each with one rectangular chapel and a short square-ended choir. The north aisle, of Transitional style, came first in *c.*1195 followed by the west front in the very early thirteenth century. The oddly placed towers and screened windows are found nowhere else in Britain. The main body of the nave owes a considerable debt to Lincoln, although now that is clearest in the transepts inspired by the design of St Hugh's choir. The building was substantially complete by 1230.

The choir and transepts were demolished in 1570, but the nave was retained as the parish church of the Canongate burgh. In the east bay of the south aisle was the Royal Vault which is now empty of its tombs. Only the wall ribs survive of the ceiling vault. The ceiling vaulting was rare inasmuch as it was sexpartite in design. In their original state, the western turrets were fashioned in a similar way to those at Lindisfarne priory. The surviving tower is lavishly decorated with blind arcading. Both towers had an additional storey capped by a short spire. The west windows are vast in area.

South of the south transept was the polygonal chapter house with a central column, and the cloister lay south of the nave. The surviving base is thirteenth-century.

In 1559, the altars of the abbey church were destroyed by the Reformers, and thereafter the abbey buildings were allowed to decay. Major repairs were made to the church before Charles I's coronation at Holyrood in 1633. Cromwellian soldiers did further damage to the church in 1650 among other things causing a destructive fire. In 1688, new fittings which had been added to the abbey church were destroyed by a Protestant mob and at the same time the Jesuit college was sacked. In 1906, it was proposed that the abbey church might be used as the Chapel of the Order of the Thistle (this is now in St Giles, High Kirk), but the proposal was rejected on account of the damage that would be done to historic fabric. Of course, there is now great symbolism in the abbey standing just across the road from the Scottish parliament building.

Above: The nave.

IONA ABBEY

ona is somewhere with great resonances for both Scotland and England. It was to Iona that St Columba came from his home in Letterkenny in north western Ireland to set up his monastery in the Inner Hebrides; it was from Iona whence came St Aidan, answering the call of King Oswald of Northumbria to come and help bring the Christian gospel to his kingdom. The combination of the setting, the climate, often softened by the winds of the Gulf Stream, and 1,500 years of Christian history still create a unique feeling on the island. As commentators often say, the atmosphere is 'thin', especially to those with a religious sensibility – the rumour of angels is never far away.

Tradition has it that it was in 563 that Columba made his journey, in a coracle with other monks, to found the earliest monastery on Iona. This was part of the Gaelic kingdom of Dal Riata. Of course, others will have come later and especially Norse invaders from Scandinavia, who set up the Kingdom of the Isles. Columba brought with him a different tradition to that brought by the Roman missionaries under Augustine and Paulinus, although, of course, even the Irish tradition had originally come from mainland continental Europe, with roots back to Rome. Nonetheless, differences did exist – in tonsure, on the dating of Easter and the ambient culture, and these far isles did not accept the Roman pattern until the early eighth century. The Book of Kells may have been produced here at the end of that century.

Columba's monastery would almost certainly have been built of wood and no trace of it survives. In the twelfth century, however, the abbey was refounded as a Benedictine house and in front of the abbey stands the ninth-century St Martin's Cross. Other eighth-century crosses survive. The Benedictine church appears to have been cruciform, the north and south transepts having chapels recessed into their east walls. The church was extended in the thirteenth century and then again later. It gained a mitred abbot in 1247 and in the sixteenth century became the Cathedral of the Isles. After the Reformation, both church and conventual buildings decayed.

Interest continued in the eighteenth century, and Johnson and Boswell's visit is vividly described! With the onset of the Romantic Movement, Walter Scott, Keats and Wordsworth all came here. In 1899, the 8th Duke of Argyll inspired the restoration of the abbey and the cathedral and priory were transferred to the new Iona Cathedral Trust. It was the vision of George Macleod, however, in setting up the Iona Community, that spurred the rebuilding especially under the architect Ian Lindsay. In 1959, Lindsay reconstructed the entire cloister – his reconstruction had, in fact, begun in 1938 with the eastern range. The late twelfth/early thirteenth-century Michael Chapel survives east of the north end of the east range.

The achievement of the rebuilding is remarkable as is the breadth of humanity of the community established here which continues to thrive.

Below: The rebuilt abbey.

SWEETHEART ABBEY

et within Galloway, and thus within that part of Scotland where Bede suggests St Ninian established his missionary base, at Whithorn, as early as the fourth century, Sweetheart Abbey was, ironically, the last of the medieval abbeys established in Scotland. It was Devorgilla, Lady of Galloway and the widow of John Balliol, who aimed to found an abbey here in *c.*1270. A commission from the Cistercian General Chapter commissioned the Abbots of Furness and Rievaulx to examine the proposed site and they found in favour. Buildings may well have begun being constructed *c.*1273. It was named in Latin 'Dulce Cor' or 'Sweetheart' because of Devorgilla's great devotion to her husband, whose heart, it is said was embalmed and at her death, in 1289, it was buried in her grave in the choir of the abbey church.

The abbey was established as a daughter house to nearby Dundrennan. Happily, extensive ruins of the abbey survive – it is one of the most complete survivals of a monastic church in Scotland, due largely to the energies of local lairds in the eighteenth century. Sadly, all the conventual buildings are gone. The lofty tower of the church is the identifying feature in the adjacent village of New Abbey. The nave, including its arcades and clerestory, survives almost complete. Built of warm red ashlar sandstone, it is of particular interest since it was begun in the early fourteenth century when few other churches were being built in Scotland. The grant of the land

from Buittle parish was made by Sir Archibald Douglas ('the Grim!') in 1369. By this time the abbey had been at least partially wrecked by lightning. Building resumed in the late fourteenth century.

The church has an aisled nave of six bays similar to Dundrennan. There is a crossing whose arches still survive, supporting the tower. The transepts have eastern chapels and there is an unaisled three-bay presbytery. The west front includes a gable for the nave but not for the ends of the aisles. Above the door and porch is an enormous pointed arch, culminating in sculpted human figures. The nave clerestory rises from what would have been the ridges of the lost aisle roofs. The south transept largely survives as does much of the north transept. There is a large sarcophagus monument in the south transept of 1931–3. The interior of the church also feels fairly complete. There is no triforium and this had been in common with many early Cistercian churches.

Of the claustral buildings, apart from the lower courses of the walls of the eastern range, there is little to be seen. The south range as was usual largely devoted to the refectory and kitchens – a fragment of a round-arched doorway remains. There are substantial remains too of the precinct walls.

Following the Reformation, the church was abandoned and the estate became part of a barony, but in 1779, local gentlemen bought the abbey church in the hope of preserving it, although little work appears to have been done.

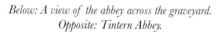

Below: A view of the abbey across the graveyard.
Opposite: Tintern Abbey.

WALES

For many, over the centuries, it has been the location of so many of the Welsh abbeys and priories that has drawn people to them, and especially as the psychology behind the 'Grand Tour' gained in momentum. The Romantic movement added its weight to this and J.M.W. Turner's watercolours, alongside the poetry of Wordsworth and others, capture this fascination. Once again, in Wales, the history of monastic life goes back well into the mists of time. The pattern of obscure local saints matches that of Cornwall, and the early Celtic monk-missionaries laid the foundations. David, and Patrick, who was later 'exported' to Ireland, are perhaps the two most famous witnesses to this. The encounter of this ancient observance with the Roman tradition in the person of Augustine on the banks of the River Severn was not an encouraging one! The Norman conquest did its work in bringing Romanesque architecture and wider mainland continental links within religious orders. The wars with England and the rebellion of Owain Glyndwr ironically brought both destruction but also the development of later architectural styles. Later still, in the south particularly, the industrial revolution wrought its own havoc, although more recently both old and new have survived, complementing each other's contribution to contemporary culture.

TINTERN ABBEY

Cadw's purple prose introductio to one of its most admired sites runs thus: 'Tintern Abbey is a national icon – still standing in roofless splendour on the banks of the River Wye nearly 500 years since its tragic fall from grace.' A favourite scene for portrait painters, including J.M.W. Turner's well known landscape, with its light effect redolent of the artist's later work. It is perhaps most famously immortalised in Wordsworth's 'Lines composed a few miles above Tintern Abbey', which do not mention the abbey but nevertheless recall an earlier visit,

'And this green pastoral landscape, were to me
More dear, both for themselves and for thy sake.'

Wordsworth's love of nature and his religious impulses come together here uniquely caught by the glory of the wider landscape. It is the best preserved medieval abbey in Wales

The abbey, the first Cistercian foundation in Wales, was founded in 1131 by Walter de Clare, the Marcher Lord of Chepstow. It is whimsically said of Abbot Henry, a reformed robber, that he was better

known for his crying at the altar than for his architectural ambitions, but then the 'gift of tears' was not unknown among mystics in medieval times.

The first building at Tintern was of timber, with a simple stone church and modest cloister following later. Sitting near to the village of Tintern, it stands in Monmouthshire, just on the border with Gloucestershire in England, and at the point where the Wye ceases to be tidal. As with all Cistercian monasteries, there were both priests and lay brothers. The lay brothers who were largely illiterate were crucial since the order was committed to both prayer and work.

Fairly rare among Cistercian abbeys, the present church was built later in the Decorated style, it is 70 metres (230 feet) high and 50 metres (165 feet) wide. The sacristy, chapter house, refectory, kitchen and parlour all survive, giving one a clear sense of the plan of the monastery and the pattern of life of the monks. The lay brothers quarters can also still be seen. As has been hinted the remains that we can see are the product of a long period of building, some 400 years between 1138 and the Dissolution in 1536. Of the first building little remains as the

Below: The nave and crossing.

Above: Viewed from the north.

reconstruction was complete – only two cupboards in the cloisters and some pieces of walling are from the earlier building. The rebuilding, starting in 1269, continued throughout the thirteenth century with the church being built between 1269 and 1301, when the abbey was again consecrated. The later Lord of Chepstow, the then Duke of Norfolk, Roger Bigod was a generous benefactor. The plan is cruciform with an aisled nave and two chapels in each transept. It is built of mellow-coloured Old Red Sandstone. The nave is of six bays and the presbytery four bays. The width of the cloister was increased in the thirteenth century forming almost a square. Although the lay brothers' refectory remains, their dormitory, which was above, has been lost. The abbot's lodgings were also rebuilt in the fourteenth century. The west front has a magnificent seven-lancet window.

Tintern has been celebrated over the past three centuries, as the profusion of art and literature which it has begotten suggest – tourism in the Wye valley is not new! The abbey appears in a number of essays written by tourists in both the eighteenth and nineteenth centuries. Samuel Taylor Coleridge famously just avoided riding his horse over the edge of a quarry nearby. The abbey was bought by the Duke of Beaufort for the Crown in 1901 and Cadw have administered it since 1984. Apart from Turner's landscape, Thomas Gainsborough painted the abbey, as did John Piper in the twentieth century.

CALDEY ISLAND

Just off the coast of South West Wales, near Tenby, lies Caldey Island, one of Britain's holy islets. In the summer months boats ply from Tenby to the island for day visits. It has been inhabited for at least 10,000 years throughout the Stone and Bronze Ages. In the sixth century, it became known as Ynys Byr or Pyro's Island, after the first known abbot. The tenth century saw the end of the Celtic settlement – the name Caldey has Norse roots. Monasticism returned to the island in the twelfth century following the Norman conquest. Benedictine monks from Tiron in Normandy established an outpost of St Dogmael's, which they had founded in North Pembrokeshire. The community remained until the Dissolution in 1536. Their former domicile is still known as The Old Priory.

In 1906, a group of Anglican Benedictines came and restored St David's church, and in 1913, the entire community converted to Roman Catholicism. In 1925, the island was sold to a Cistercian community from Scourmont Abbey in Belgium who arrived here in 1929, re-establishing the Welsh

Cistercian tradition, following the stricter Trappist rule. The abbey is an excellent example of Arts and Crafts architecture – perhaps the best in Wales. The abbey itself is not open to the public but there is a shop selling products of the abbey.

Above: The modern abbey at Caldey Island.

LLANTHONY ABBEY

Turner's atmospheric watercolour of Llanthony captures the romanticism of the site perfectly. The turbulent River Honddu sets the scene. Giraldus Cambrensis captured this in words: 'Here is a site truly suited to the monastic life . . . in a wilderness removed from the bustle of mankind.' The location is dramatic on the edge of the Black Mountains which are the background to this unforgettable ruin. The origins of the priory date back to 1100, when Walter de Lacy came upon a ruined chapel dedicated to St David here and was inspired to adopt a life of study and devotion. Hermits then came here first in *c.*1103 and by *c.*1109, the beginnings of monastic life were established. By 1118, there were forty monks forming a community of Augustinian Canons Regular, living in what has become known as Llanthony Primo.

The beginnings were not without incident. Continued attacks from the local Welsh population caused the monks to retire to Gloucester in 1135, but by *c.*1186, another member of the de Lacy family endowed the estate with revenues from his Irish property holdings. Further gifts came from Adam de Freypo and Geoffrey de Cusack, also from Ireland. This allowed building to begin. The church was built towards the end of the century with the choir, transepts and central tower coming first, followed by the aisled nave and western towers. The style is austere Early English and Transitional. The arcades are of the plainest simplest arches. The number of monks was reduced following the construction of Llanthony Secunda.

Llanthony Secunda became one of the great medieval buildings of Wales. Renewed building began *c.*1325 with a new gatehouse. On Palm Sunday in April 1327, the deposed Edward II stayed at the priory on his journey to Berkeley Castle where it is said he was murdered. The buildings were abandoned in 1538 with the Dissolution, and they gradually declined. Few of the claustral buildings survive to any height, although the small infirmary chapel became and remains the parish church. At the turn of the eighteenth century, Sir Mark Wood of Chepstow bought the estate converting some of the buildings into a house and shooting box.

The buildings, however, have never ceased to cast their spell. In 1807, Walter Savage Landor, the poet, bought the abbey from Wood. Through an Act of Parliament, Landor was allowed to demolish some of Wood's buildings, and then constructed a house which he never completed. A nearby avenue of trees is still known as Landor's Larches. Famously, Landor described the beauty of the place, all the way down to nightingales and glow-worms to his friend, the poet, Robert Southey. Later, Landor's fairly grandiose plans fell to bits, leading to squabbles and eventually to court action after which he abandoned the estate, leaving his mother to pay his creditors!

The next individual to embark upon what would turn out to be an unfinished project, inspired by Llanthony's dramatic beauty, was Joseph Leycester Lyne, known as Father Ignatius. He felt called to revive the Benedictine life in the Church of England. Having attempted to buy the ruins and having been thwarted, instead he set up his own monastery at Capel-y-Ffin, just three miles away. The foundation lasted until Ignatius' death in 1908, although the community did not grow healthily and there were many tensions. The sculptor Eric Gill also tried to buy the estate and lived there for some time but he had to be content with the poorly built monastery of Ignatius. The poet and artist, David Jones, also lived here with Gill and his family. Landor's lasting inheritance is the hotel which took over the house built by the poet.

Below: The abbey in its dramatic setting.

MARGAM ABBEY

Margam is perhaps now most famous outside Wales for its huge steel works next door, which lies between Margam itself and Port Talbot. It is an ancient settlement and the Cistercian abbey was founded in 1147 as a daughter house of Clairvaux by Robert, Earl of Gloucester. Early Celtic style crosses, however, point to a previous much earlier foundation. The third abbot, one Conan, was celebrated by the historian Giraldus Cambrensis, often known simply as Gerald of Wales. Conan contributed to Patristic literature.

The nave of the abbey survives intact and there are further remains of the conventual buildings including the surprisingly capacious twelve-sided chapter house, dating from the thirteenth century. The abbey undercroft also survives. On the hill just across from the abbey are the ruins of another of the monastic buildings known as Capel Mair ar y Bryn, meaning simply, the chapel of St Mary on the hill. This unusual survivor is thought to have been built so that the monks tending the monastic flock of sheep would not have to return to the abbey itself to attend the offices at the main church. The monastery was closed at the Dissolution in 1536, but the nave survived, as it does to the present day, as the parish church.

Above: The chapter house.

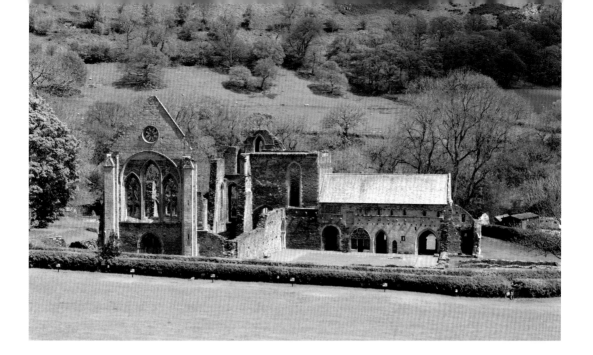

VALLE CRUCIS ABBEY

Set in a beautiful valley, the 'valley of the cross' in Llantysilio near Llangollen, the abbey presents an unforgettable landscape. It is now in the hands of Cadw who, in their introduction to the monument, note that 'Valle Crucis was truly Welsh from the moment it was founded by Prince Madog ap Gruffyd and the white monks of the Cistercian order'. Monks had names like Tudur and Hywel. Madog was buried in the abbey upon his death in 1236 and the abbey buildings were complete by that date. The abbey stands against steep hills and the high gables of the east end of the church are silhouetted against this. The ninth-century pillar of Eliseg, a Welsh chieftain, stands nearby and gives the valley its name.

When it was established in 1201, it was the last of the Welsh Cistercian abbeys to be built. It was effectively a daughter house of the abbey at Strata Marcella, located on the west bank of the River Severn near Welshpool – and began with just twelve monks. Eventually the completed abbey comprised a community of around sixty brothers, twenty of whom were monks and forty lay brothers. The abbey did not have an easy time, following a serious fire at one point and then, as it was caught up in the English-Welsh wars in the reign of Edward I of England in the early thirteenth century. Almost certainly, it was further damaged in Owain Glendwr's rebellion in 1400. In more peaceful times, in the later fifteenth century, it was the home of a number of Welsh poets.

The monastic church was probably begun immediately after the foundation in 1201. It was a cruciform building and both the east and west fronts survive, including the masonry of a rose window. The east end had simple lancets but the west end had two light traceried windows together with the rose window above. The east end was restored by Sir Gilbert Scott in 1870. In the fourteenth century, the church was divided by a pulpitum, separating the monks church from that of the lay brothers. Only the bases of the nave pillars along with fragments of the north transept or aisles but much more in the south transept and south aisles.

Of the conventual buildings, the east range is mainly intact – the west range with the lay brothers' frater has been lost, and the southern range with the monks' frater is also ruinous. The chapter house is a splendid space with a rib vault rising from four columns with no capitals. The only surviving Welsh monastic fishpond is here at Valle Crucis. Parts of the dormitory and abbot's lodgings, on the first floor are accessible to the public.

The abbey was closed with the Dissolution in 1537, with the building being given by Henry VIII to Sir William Puckering. By the end of the sixteenth century, the south range had been converted into a manor house. Hester Puckering married Edward, 1st Baron Wotton and so the abbey passed by marriage into the Wotton family.

Above: The ruins of Valle Crucis Abbey.

NEATH ABBEY

n the twentieth century, Neath was known perhaps most of all as a centre of industry based on coal mining and iron and copper smelting works. The abbey itself was engulfed in this and became industrial premises. Neath is, however, an ancient town, as both the ruins of its castle and those of the abbey testify. Indeed, the sheer extent of the ruins are a breathtaking sight. They are among the most important monastic ruins in south east Wales.

The abbey was founded for Savigniac monks in 1111, but in 1147, the Savigniac congregations were merged with the Cistercian order. It became the largest abbey in Wales, having been founded formally by Richard I de Greville, who was one of the twelve knights of Glamorgan, who gave his estate of some 8,000 acres to the Savigniac monks of western Normandy. The monks first arrived in 1130. The lay brothers' accommodation dates from the late twelfth century, although the two chimneys on the east wall are from industrial furnaces. The church was rebuilt in the thirteenth and fourteenth centuries. Much of the west front of the monastic church survives with

the nave aisle walls. Fragments of the transepts and their chapels remain, with part of the night stair clearly visible.

Little of the cloister is there but its plan is set out with the entrances to the chapter house and refectory in their usual places. Almost miraculously some very fine medieval tiles survive. The finest fragment of all is the dorter undercroft, a splendid room with a quadripartite vault rising from elegant round columns, and with an enormous fireplace. This was originally a room for the novices. North of the abbey ruins is the rather sad thirteenth/fourteenth-century gatehouse, in which are preserved two pointed windows, alongside a stretch of the thirteenth-century abbey walls.

Most remarkable of all is how much of the abbey has been preserved, allowing for the later history, which is not far short of bizarre. As with many similar buildings, following the Dissolution in 1539, the abbot's lodgings were converted, at the end of the sixteenth century, into a grand Tudor mansion at the centre of what became a substantial estate, owned by

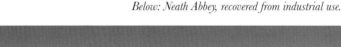

Below: Neath Abbey, recovered from industrial use.

Above: An aerial view of Neath Abbey.

Sir John Herbert. The mansion only served as a private residence for about 100 years, as the next still more improbable page of history was turned.

Uniquely, as the industrial revolution unfolded, the abbey became the centre of heavy industry. In the early eighteenth century, the ruins of the abbey began to be used for smelting. Two smelting furnaces were built into the lay brothers' range and industry engulfed the church spreading throughout the ruins. The grand mansion of the Herberts became tenements for workers and their families. Salvation came later, when Lord Dynevor inherited the site, and welcomed archaeologists on to the site. Between 1923 and 1935 4,000 tons of debris were removed from the abbey grounds. A tablet in the south transept captures this, as it remembers Glen Arthur Taylor FSA, who led the work of the Neath Abbey Research Party in recovering the stone work of this great building.

GLOSSARY

Words within entries set in **bold** type are themselves defined elsewhere.

AISLE in a church, either the areas either side of the **nave**, separated from it by pillars, or a passage running between the rows of seats

AMBULATORY in a monastery, a **cloister** or place for walking. Often covered and making use of **arcading**

APSE a rounded recess with a domed roof, often situated at the end of the **choir**, **aisles** or **nave** of a church

ARCADING decoration by means of a series of arches

AUGUSTINIAN of the order of St Augustine of Hippo

AUMBRY locker or recess in a church wall in which sacramental vessels are stored

BALDACHINO a canopy, usually over an altar or a tomb, supported by columns

BARREL VAULT a vault with a semi-cylindrical roof

BAPTISTRY separate building containing the font

BASILICA a rectangular hall with two rows of columns and an **apse** at the end

BENEDICTINE of the order of St Benedict

BOSS an ornament fixed at the intersection of the arches which supports a **rib vault**

BUTTRESS a structure built against a wall to support it, for example a **flying buttress**

CARMELITE of the order of Our Lady of Mount Carmel

CELLARER the officer of a monastery in charge of the cellar

CENSER a container in which incense is burned

CHANCEL the part of a church used by clergy and choir, to the east of the **nave** and **transepts**

CHANTRY a small chapel

CHAPTER HOUSE a building, often separate, used for meetings of a cathedral or monastic chapter

CHEVET apsidal end to a church with an ambulatory giving access to radial chapels around the apse

CHOIR or **QUIRE** that part of a church where the church choir and clergy sit

CISTERCIAN an off-shoot of the Benedictine order, founded at Cîteaux in France in the late eleventh century

CLERESTORY the upper part of a large church, above the level of the roofs of the aisles, where windows let light into the central parts of the church

CLOISTERS covered passages connecting the church to other parts of a monastery

CLOSE the enclosed area around a cathedral

CLUNIAC of the branch of the Benedictine order founded at Cluny in France in the early tenth century

CROSSING the part of a cathedral where the **nave** intersects with the transept

CRYPT a subterranean cell, chapel or chamber that is usually vaulted

CURVILINEAR style of window design of the late **Decorated** period featuring flowing patterns of **tracery**

DECORATED architectural period (1307–77) which was characterised by the use of wider windows, projecting **buttresses**, tall pinnacles, and the rapid development of window **tracery** through the **Geometric** and **Curvilinear** styles

DOGTOOTH decoration within arcading in **Romanesque** and some **Early English** buildings

DOMINICAN of the order of St Dominic

DORTER a monastic dormitory

EARLY ENGLISH architecture of the earliest phase of the **Gothic** period

FAN VAULTING a highly decorative and complex type of vaulting of the later **Gothic** period

FERETORY a shrine for relics used in procession

FLÈCHE a slim spire that rises from the point at which the **nave** and **transepts** intersect

FLYING BUTTRESS a prop built out from a pier or other support and supporting the main structure

FRANCISCAN of the order of St Francis of Assisi

FRONT in architecture, any side of a building, usually the one where the entrance is sited

GALILEE western porch in certain churches where traditionally penitents would wait before making their confession

GEOMETRIC a style of window design used in the early **Decorated** period centring on geometric shapes used mainly in the fourteenth century. It later developed into the more flowing **Curvilinear** style

GOTHIC architectural style prevalent in Western Europe from the twelfth to fifteenth centuries. It is characterised by the use of pointed archways

GRISAILLE a particular method of decorative painting on walls or ceilings

HOSTRY equivalent to 'hostelry' and related to 'hospital' and 'hotel', the word basically signifies a place where guests could stay

LANCET WINDOW high, narrow window with a pointed top

LAUDIAN the period in the seventeenth century during William Laud's archiepiscopate at Canterbury, and often referring to a full altar cloth of that period

LIERNE rib vaulting of the **Gothic** period in which the ribs cross each other

LOCUTORY part of a monastery set apart for meeting and conversation

MISERICORD a tip-up seat in a church with a projecting shelf on the underside, designed to support those standing at prayer for long periods

NARTHEX a vestibule between the cathedral entrance and the **nave**

NAVE the main part of a church, running from the main door to the **choir** in a west–east direction

NICHE a shallow recess in a wall for displaying a statue or other ornament

PARLATORIUM a room, normally off the cloister, where monks might relax and talk with each other – effectively a common room

PERPENDICULAR architectural style (1377–1485), a phase of the **Gothic** period, when the designs of the **Decorated** period developed into longer, taller and more linear forms

PIER in architecture, a solid masonry support which sustains vertical pressure

PRESBYTERY the part of a church beyond the **choir** at the east end, where only the clergy would enter

PULPITUM a large stone or wooden screen or gallery between the **nave** and the **choir**

QUATREFOIL in architecture, an ornament in the form of a ring of four leaves or petals

QUIRE *see* **CHOIR**

REFECTORY the dining room of a monastery

RELIQUARY a small box or shrine for holy relics (the mortal remains of saints)

REREDORTER a monastic communal latrine

REREDOS a decorative screen or painting behind the altar

RESPOND a long, narrow column supporting arches and ribs, mainly in **Gothic** buildings

RETABLE either a shelf for ornaments or a frame for decorative panels, found behind the altar of a church

RETRO-CHOIR or **RETRO-QUIRE** the parts of a large church behind the high altar

RIB VAULT a vault built with 'ribs' or arches which support the roof

ROMANESQUE prevalent style of buildings erected in Europe between Roman times and the rise of **Gothic** style in the twelfth century

TRACERY ornamental stonework in **Gothic** windows

TRANSEPT the part of a cruciform church which crosses the **nave** in a north–south direction; also each of its two arms (i.e. the north and south transepts)

TRANSITIONAL architecture of the period *c.*1145–*c.*1190, when there was a gradual transition from **Romanesque** to Early **Gothic**

TRIBUNE GALLERY a raised gallery of seats

TRIFORIUM a gallery or arcade in the wall situated over the arches at the sides of the **nave** and **choir**

TURRET a small tower which forms part of the structure of a larger building

TYMPANUM the space between door lintel and arch

UNDERCROFT a crypt or vault below the floor of a church

INDEX

PICTURE CREDITS